MERCY PILOT

The Joe Crosson Story

DIRK TORDOFF

EPICENTER PRESS

Epicenter Press is a regional press founded in Alaska whose interests include but are not limited to the arts, history, environment, and diverse cultures and lifestyles of the Pacific Northwest and high latitudes. We seek both the traditional and innovative in publishing nonfiction books, and contemporary art and photography giftbooks.

Publisher: Kent Sturgis
Editor: Don Graydon
Cover and Book Design: Elizabeth Watson, Watson Graphics
Maps: Marge Mueller, Gray Mouse Graphics
Proofreader: Sherrill Carlson
Index: Sherrill Carlson
Printer: Transcontinental Printing

Library of Congress Control Number 2002111723
ISBN 0-9708493-7-0

Booksellers: This title is available from major wholesalers. Retail discounts are available from our trade distributor, Graphic Arts Center Publishing Co., PO Box 10306, Portland, OR 97210. Phone 800-452-3032.

PRINTED IN CANADA

First Edition
First Printing, September 2002

10 9 8 7 6 5 4 3 2 1

To order single copies of MERCY PILOT, mail $17.95 plus $4.95 for shipping (WA residents add $2.00 state sales tax) to: Epicenter Press, PO Box 82368, Kenmore, WA 98028.

Discover exciting ALASKA BOOK ADVENTURES! Visit our online Alaska bookstore and art gallery at www.EpicenterPress.com, or call our 24-hour, toll-free hotline at 800-950-6663

DEDICATION

To you Mom, for your faith in me.

To you Lillian, for keeping the story alive.

And to you Cathie, it wouldn't have

happened without you.

ACKNOWLEDGMENTS

ALTHOUGH MANY OF Joe Crosson's accomplishments were well documented, very little was ever put in print about his personality and character. Writing about his human side was a challenge, but many people helped in a variety of ways. This book wouldn't have been possible without the help of the family, employees, and friends of Joe Crosson.

Lillian Crosson and her children Joe Jr., Don, Bob, and Sue all helped with logistics and support during my many trips to Seattle to research and index Lillian's incredible collection of aviation memorabilia. They also talked freely about their memories of family life.

Kay Kennedy started me in this direction and encouraged me in the beginning. Burt Armstrong, Gene Rogge, Ruth Olson, Joanne Tolefson, Jean Potter Marsh, and Jim Hutchison all gave me their time and priceless interviews about life in Fairbanks and aviation, and personal glimpses of Joe.

Bob Gleason allowed me to interview him extensively and reviewed the manuscript on several occasions until it was accurate. His memories are amazingly sharp and his advice was superb.

Helen Atkinson shared memories of working with Joe, reviewed the manuscript, and was a never-ending source of encouragement and support during the entire process.

Richard Wien thought the project was worthwhile and reviewed early drafts with a sense of history. Chris Matthews, Dr. James Cerney, and Tom George also read the manuscript with the sharp eyes of pilots. Sharon McLeod-Everette and Dr. Curtis Kimball also reviewed the manuscript at different stages of development and offered encouragement.

My sons Spencer and Graham not only put up with my hours of research and writing, but they also helped me with computer applications and positive encouragement during the process, and reminded me to stop and enjoy life along the way.

My wife, Cathie, who helped in all aspects of the book, always supported this project, even in my personal times of doubt.

Thanks to all of you, and to those whose efforts I have inadvertently missed.

CONTENTS

PREFACE

I FIRST KNEW Joe Crosson the way most people know celebrities. To me, he was a name, a face, a series of accomplishments. He was one of the famous pilots and Alaska heroes whose names and exploits were topics of conversation for the adults during my boyhood in Fairbanks. I knew Crosson was an early bush pilot who brought the bodies of Wiley Post and Will Rogers back from Barrow in the 1930s; I knew that he flew biplanes in the winter, that he always helped people in trouble, and that there was a street named for him. That's about all I knew.

As I studied at the University of Alaska Fairbanks, my appreciation for Joe Crosson began to grow. A portrait of Joe's handsome, smiling face greeted me each time I approached the Alaska and Polar Regions Archives at the Rasmuson Library. Researching the 1920s in Alaska brought me unexpectedly face to face with the image of Joe's beautiful sister Marvel, who also flew in Alaska way back then.

My curiosity was further piqued quite by accident as I was researching the 1926 flight of the dirigible *Norge*. While passing a desk in the archives office, an open photo album caught my eye. In it were crystal-clear pictures of the *Norge* on the ice at Teller, Alaska. There were also pictures of a biplane and a young pilot. It was Joe Crosson, a boyish version of the aviator whose portrait smiled at me in the library. I wanted to know more about him, and I started looking.

To my amazement there was little in print on Crosson. He occupied one chapter in Jean Potter's *The Flying North*, written during World War II, and his role in the 1930 search for missing pilot Ben Eielson was detailed in Bob Gleason's *Icebound in the Siberian Arctic*. More of Joe's early Alaskan adventures were detailed in Bob Stevens' *Alaskan Aviation History* and a tiny bit more about Marvel surfaces, but that volume ends in 1930. There was no biography on Joe and even less in print on Marvel, so I went back to that scrapbook I'd seen in the archives.

The archivist told me the scrapbook was on loan from Joe's widow, Lillian Crosson, who was alive and well at her home in Seattle, and brimming with great stories of the past. It seemed too good to be true. But after a few phone calls and several months, I was in Lillian's home in Seattle.

Over the next several years I made numerous trips to Seattle to learn the story firsthand from Lillian and from her collection of Alaska aviation history. Lillian had saved every picture and scrap of paper that covered the careers of her husband, Joe, and of Marvel, who became her best friend. The story that unfolded was one of excitement and sadness, of first flights and final journeys, of triumph and tragedy, of kindness and of love—love for flying, love for family, and love of life.

From the first landing on a Mount McKinley glacier to Antarctic flights, from survival epics to rescue missions, from pioneering journeys in open-cockpit biplanes to modern aircraft, this story was too good to be kept a secret; it needed to be shared with people who prize aviation, history, and Alaska.

A book can't possibly cover the entire life of a man, and trying to chose the high points in the career of an Alaska bush pilot was a great challenge. Joe Crosson died before I was born, but I have enjoyed getting to know his family and his story. I hope you do, too.

Joe in Fairbanks, Alaska

INTRODUCTION

IN THE EARLY 1900S, flying was starting to come of age. But the sky remained the domain of the bravest souls willing to risk life and limb in noisy, rickety craft to soar above the nonbelievers.

Aviators were larger than life. They accomplished feats nearly inconceivable to the world only a little while before. The "firsts" began to fall: first passenger flight, first to reach 10,000 feet, first across the English Channel, first transcontinental flight. Local celebrities of aviation rose to national and international acclaim as their achievements mounted. Orville and Wilbur Wright, Glenn Curtiss, Harriet Quimbey, and Louis Bleriot appeared regularly in the headlines. Their exploits encouraged many young people to be among the first in the air, to go higher, faster, and farther than those before them.

In those early years of the twentieth century, the United States was shrinking. Roads connected most towns, telegraph and telephones provided nearly instantaneous communication, railroads allowed travel or shipping cross-country. And aviation made time and space shrink faster.

No place in the world was more primed for the benefits of flying than the Territory of Alaska. Many of the nation's travel and communication advances were unknown in this wild land more than

◄ Joe sits in the pilot's seat of the ungainly Fokker F.III in Fairbanks, an odd craft that was ill-suited to Alaska aviation.

twice the size of Texas. Stern-wheel riverboats made summer trips upstream, but other transportation was limited to horse-drawn stages on a few dirt roads hacked from the wilderness—and only during about a three-month window when the absence of snow, water, and mud allowed. Most winter travel was accomplished by dogsled or horse-drawn sledge, and walking was often still the most reliable way to get from here to there.

The number one industry in Interior Alaska was gold mining. Miners and prospectors traveled through thick forests, across rivers, and through swamps and fields of tussocks to their claims. A hundred-mile trip could take a week or more. More than one miner looked skyward and envied the geese and ducks as they flew overhead, far above the miserable trails and the millions of mosquitoes, no-see-ums, and biting flies that plagued ground travelers.

▼ *Marvel Crosson*

Aviation changed Alaska for everyone. After arrival of the airplane, a miner with a broken leg faced only a few hours of travel to medical help instead of days. The life of a sick child in a river village could be saved by flying her to a doctor. Eskimos in Kotzebue could eat fresh oranges in the winter. And at Barrow, news from loved ones in Fairbanks could be delivered in a day, instead of a month.

It wasn't the machinery that made the difference, it was the aviators. These daring pioneers of the northern skies saved lives, saved time, and were the closest things to angels many of the people of Alaska ever saw. And one of the first was a handsome young man who knew from the age of ten that his destiny lay in aviation.

Joe Crosson was born in Kansas, raised in Colorado, learned to fly in California, and died in Seattle. But his life was in Alaska.

At his birth, family and friends would have been astounded to know how his life would turn out, about the dream he would share with his sister Marvel, and where that dream would take them.

Joe and Marvel led lives that at first were ordinary, but rose to extraordinary on the wings of the fledgling industry of aviation, in which they achieved fame and became role models for a generation of flyers. Brother and sister enjoyed both the adulation that accompanies tremendous success and suffered the heartbreak that comes from life-shattering tragedy.

As a famous flyer, Joe made friends ranging from backwoods prospectors to celebrities like Hap Arnold, Eddie Rickenbacker, Billy Mitchell, Jimmy Doolittle, Sir Hubert Wilkins, and Vilhjalmur Stefansson. His flying took him throughout the United States and to both ends of the Earth.

Marvel's image graced newspapers and magazines, with a smile and story that thrilled millions. Flying in Alaska, setting altitude records, and racing airplanes was most unusual for a young lady in the 1920s.

▲ *Joe in front of the Fokker F.III.*

Joe Crosson was a true Alaska pioneer, but not of the pick-and-shovel variety of the mining camps. His tools were propellers and wings. When he arrived in Alaska, the aviation industry was just a fledgling. He played a big part in establishing regular flights in the territory and linking Alaska by air to the rest of the United States and the world.

Villagers greeting Joe's airplane for the first time forever remembered his smile, and from his plane he became the first to gaze upon vistas now cherished by all. Whether delivering lifesaving serum to remote villages, searching for lost pilots, or returning the shattered bodies of close friends or national heroes to their families, the mercy pilot left an enduring record of courage and accomplishment.

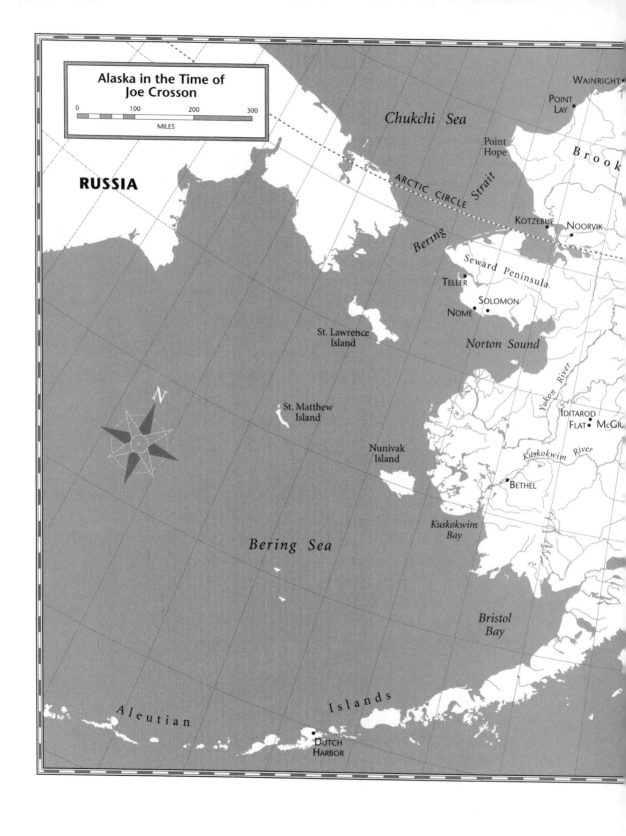

Alaska in the Time of
Joe Crosson

0   100   200   300
MILES

RUSSIA

Chukchi Sea

WAINRIGHT

POINT
LAY

Point
Hope

Brook

ARCTIC CIRCLE

Strait

KOTZEBUE   NOORVIK

Bering

Seward Peninsula

TELLER

SOLOMON

NOME

Norton Sound

St. Lawrence
Island

Yukon River

IDITAROD
FLAT   McGR

N

St. Matthew
Island

Kuskokwim   River

Nunivak
Island

BETHEL

Kuskokwim
Bay

Bering Sea

Bristol
Bay

Aleutian   Islands

DUTCH
HARBOR

Joe and Marvel

1

THE FLYING CROSSONS

Colorado, 1913. Joe Crosson was ten years old and his sister Marvel was thirteen when they saw an airplane for the first time. The amazing flying machine was performing at the Logan County Fair at Sterling, Colorado.

Joe had been born in Kansas in 1903, three years after Marvel was born in Indiana. Their parents, Elizabeth and Esler Crosson, later moved the family to Colorado, first to Merino and then to Sterling, where brother and sister encountered the ingenious contrivance that would carry them to fame.

Years later, Marvel wrote exuberantly about that experience:

We were returning from school and naturally had no money in our pockets. There was a crowd at the fairgrounds and we sneaked along the fence until we found a hole and luck was with us. There, right in front of us, was the airplane—one of the old type with the propeller in the back. A "pusher" it was—and the pilot was in his seat.

We heard him call something out and then the motor roared louder than before and he started off. In a few seconds he was in the air! Round and round the fairgrounds he went and each time

November 16, 1913

Swiss aviator John Domenjoz loops his Bleroit aircraft above the Statue of Liberty in the first recorded performance of the aerobatics maneuver.

◄ *Partners in a dream, brother and sister Joe and Marvel Crosson launched their careers in a plane they rebuilt from a dilapidated N-9 seaplane—the Navy version of the World War I trainer known as the Jenny.*

Joe suddenly grabbed
my shoulder and began
to jump up and down.
"I'm going to be an
aviator. I'm going to be
an aviator!" he shouted.
And I agreed with him
that it was the only
thing in the world and
said I was going to be
an aviator too.

he passed us we simply caught our breaths—it was too wonderful to be real!

Joe suddenly grabbed my shoulder and began to jump up and down. "I'm going to be an aviator. I'm going to be an aviator!" he shouted. And I agreed with him that it was the only thing in the world and said I was going to be an aviator too.

Their course was set from the moment they saw this flimsy aircraft. Marvel and Joe now focused their play time on the desire to fly. Within days their mother came out of the kitchen and was shocked to see Joe and Marvel poised on top of the garage. Joe clutched an umbrella, preparing to fly off the roof. Her shrieks were enough to stifle that particular attempt, but not the dream. Their first chance to really fly did not come until 1919, six long years later.

As Marvel recalled, in that year Esler Crosson offered the family an opportunity that involved his savings. They could opt to enjoy the money with him or "fight over it after his death." Choosing the former, the Crossons, including younger daughter Zelma, embarked on a three-month driving vacation. Among the destinations was Tijuana, for Esler wanted to see Mexico. Marvel and Joe jumped at the opportunity knowing that, just across the border, San Diego was alive with flying.

During the visit in San Diego, Marvel and Joe spent a day on their own. Not too surprisingly, they ended up at Dutch Flats Flying Field. At the field they were overwhelmed. "Once there, we did not know where to begin," Marvel said later. "There were planes everywhere and pilots going about their business just as though it was the most natural thing in the world. To us it seemed simply wonderful!"

Although they didn't have enough money for a flight, business was slack and they talked a friendly pilot into taking them up. Marvel described the flight as "a nice ride for ten minutes—it seemed like ten seconds to me, I was so thrilled."

The flight had the same effect on them as the view through the fairground fence years before. Back on the ground, Joe announced: "Marvel, that settles it! We've got to have a plane."

They soon realized their biggest obstacle was location. They lived in the wrong place to learn flying. Sterling had no airfield, no airplanes, and no pilots. In addition, the town's elevation was four thousand feet, and the relatively thin air was not ideal for the low-horsepower airplane engines of that day. Learning to fly in Sterling, Joe said, would be "like trying to drive a car on a burro trail."

San Diego, on the other hand, had an airport, good weather, airplanes, and flight instructors, and it was located at sea level: perfect conditions for budding aviators. Marvel and Joe set out to persuade their parents to move to San Diego—a process Marvel described as giving their parents the "California treatment." Whatever they did must have been effective, because within a year the family made the move and Joe and Marvel were another step closer to their goal. Now they needed to learn to fly and get a plane.

▲ *Joe and Marvel Crosson stand with their parents, Elizabeth and Esler, outside the family home in San Diego, next to the fuselage of their first airplane. The whole family pitched in to rebuild the frail craft.*

Parents Esler and Elizabeth were concerned about the situation, but Esler had the final say: "If anything is going to happen to those kids, it'll happen anyhow. Let them alone—they're happy!"

∼

IN SAN DIEGO, Marvel and Joe settled down to earn the money to advance their scheme. Marvel became a clerk in a camera store, while Joe went to work in a garage. The jobs provided income, and Joe also learned valuable mechanical skills. Early flying was fraught with engine failure, which meant the skills Joe obtained in the garage would serve him well. They began the long search for an airplane, which ultimately led them to a waterfront warehouse on the outskirts of San Diego.

At the garage, Joe had heard of an airplane for sale: a dismantled N-9 seaplane that was in storage. The N-9 was the Navy version of the JN4, more commonly known as the Jenny, a World War I trainer. The owner of the N-9 had died in the crash of another airplane, and his widow was selling this craft. The price was only $150. They bought it. The plane came with some problems. It had pontoons, which would have to be converted to wheeled landing gear. The airplane was in pieces, it needed new fabric to cover wings and fuselage, and it had no motor. But it was all theirs!

Piece by piece, the plane arrived at the family home in San Diego. Parents Esler and Elizabeth were concerned about the situation, but Esler had the final say: "If anything is going to happen to those kids, it'll happen anyhow. Let them alone—they're happy!"

With their parents' blessing, Marvel and Joe spent the next several months putting every cent and every spare minute into transforming the parts and pieces into their very own airplane.

Wheels replaced pontoons, and the seaplane's old depth controls were removed. Joe and Marvel made numerous trips to Dutch Flats Flying Field to measure other planes and gather advice from aviators. At the family home, Esler removed the kitchen window so the wings and fuselage could be fed through the opening, and Marvel and her mother covered them with new fabric. Toil and hard work paid off as the airplane took shape. Joe and Marvel cut every possible expense to finish the project, but by the time the refurbishing was complete, they were broke—and the plane still lacked a motor.

They decided Joe should take flying lessons while the search

continued for a motor. That way Joe could teach Marvel to fly when their plane was completed. Money saved by delaying Marvel's lessons could be used to purchase an engine. Another customer at the garage sent Marvel and Joe on a hot trail. To their surprise, brand new but obsolete military surplus Curtiss OX-5 airplane motors were available, but with some restrictions.

▲ The near-perfect weather in San Diego allowed Joe countless days during the first half of the 1920s to hone the flying skills that served him well in Alaska.

The price was $125, far less than the $500 Joe and Marvel had anticipated, but the owner was not a fan of aviation and would only sell OX-5s for use in boats. Despite the fact they had no cash and had no intention of putting the motor in a boat, Joe and Marvel agreed to purchase one. The following morning they hocked their car for $125 and returned to pick up the motor in their father's car.

Another week of hard work and the plane sat in the yard complete with motor, ready to be started. Marvel climbed into the ship to operate the controls and Joe hand-propped the motor. Later she recalled the event:

The blast from the propeller had blown our neighbor's chickens up against the high board fence and the air was full of feathers. The poor chickens were molting and it looked as though another minute's blast would have made them naked to the breeze.

I got into the cockpit and a minute later Joe cranked the propeller. I felt the motor catch and a split second later the propeller began to whir. Then I did something I would never do again. I "gave her the gun" or opened the throttle wide and the result was glorious. The motor came to life with all its ninety horses bucking and the propeller whirled into invisibility. But Joe suddenly shouted to cut it off and I did so. He was waving his arms and seemed very excited.

I thought something had gone wrong with our beloved ship and was aghast for a second. Then I saw what had happened. The blast from the propeller had blown our neighbor's chickens up against the high board fence and the air was full of feathers. The poor chickens were molting and it looked as though another minute's blast would have made them naked to the breeze.

The neighbor charged Joe and Marvel five dollars for each chicken lost. Luckily, most of the chickens survived.

Getting the plane to an airstrip was a bit of a challenge. One midnight in May 1922, the Crossons towed the plane along deserted San Diego streets to Dutch Flats Flying Field. With the skilled help of their friends from Ryan Aircraft and Dutch Flats, the flying wires and control cables were adjusted. Joe's flight instructor, an ex-Army pilot, took it up for a trial run and it flew well. Now that they had a plane, practice was more affordable, and Joe soon got his license—signed by Orville Wright, who was chairman of the approving committee of the National Aeronautic Association of the USA, which at that time governed aviation in this country. Then it was Marvel's turn.

Joe began teaching Marvel to fly. She was a bit ahead of the game because she had been able to learn much from the pilots and mechanics at the field. They had answered her questions honestly, treating her with a degree of camaraderie. But when they found out she was actually learning to fly, they began to treat her differently.

As Marvel put it: "Those good fellows never forgot that I was a girl! There was a shade of condescension in their palship—they acted as though it were a pleasant thing for a girl to be interested in flying, but 'just among us men' it was of no importance. I could feel the sex line

◄ *Joe poses with his sisters, Marvel (left) and Zelma. Zelma never took up flying, but like Joe and Marvel, she eventually moved to Alaska.*

▶ *Young Joe Crosson spent every available hour at the Dutch Flats airfield near San Diego, learning to fly.*

drawn against me, in spite of the fact that they were splendid fellows and pals of Joe's."

Joe would have no part of this discrimination against his partner, and the pair set about proving Marvel's ability.

After she was competent in the plane, Joe had Marvel take the controls. He then stepped out on the wing as they flew over the field.

But when they landed, the men refused to believe Marvel had been flying or that Joe would risk his neck with a woman at the controls.

"Joe got peeved and we trundled the ship back to the line and took off again," Marvel recalled. "This time I flew her much lower and we shot over the hangars with Joe on the wing waving like all possessed. This time they believed I was piloting and there was a very different tone to their good-fellowship from then on. They knew how Joe felt about it—he would never get out on the wing with any other pilot but me, and they knew it."

Both Marvel and Joe won the admiration of other pilots. At home their parents were delighted. Elizabeth took Marvel in her arms and said, "Marvel, child, I'm just as proud as I can be!" Marvel also recalled that "Father did not have much to say, but his eyes twinkled and Joe heard next day that he had told some of his cronies that his girl 'could fly with the best of 'em.'"

Nine years had passed since Marvel and Joe had first seen an airplane. Now it was 1922, and they had their own airplane and knew how to fly it. Keeping it in the air was their new challenge. Marvel remembered the time fondly.

> The following years were perhaps the happiest of my life. Joe and I flew all the time—we were always in the air. Of course, we did not have any money to waste and every dollar would be translated into gas as soon as we reached the flying field. Sometimes we had only a dollar between us and would reach the field with a very limited prospect ahead of us, but we had lots of luck. Usually one of us would scare up a passenger or two and that would finance all the gas needed for several days.

For the next few years, life continued at a steady and predictable pace: Joe worked in the garage, Marvel in the camera store, and all possible money went to keep their plane in the air. Both of the young pilots wanted to do more in aviation, but opportunities to advance were rare. Then in early 1926, Joe received an invitation to come to Alaska.

"Father did not have much to say, but his eyes twinkled and Joe heard next day that he had told some of his cronies that his girl 'could fly with the best of 'em.'"

Joe with the F. III

2

NORTH TO ALASKA

San Diego, January 1926. A long telegram arrived from A. A. Bennett, pilot for the Fairbanks Airplane Corporation in Alaska, offering Joe Crosson a job. After talking it over with Marvel and with his parents, Joe was quick to accept. He and Marvel still planned to work together, but for now she would stay and fly in California while he flew farther north.

Bennett, former manager of the San Diego Airport and Flying School, had been hired in Alaska the year before. He was looking for a good pilot who was also a skilled mechanic and capable of maintaining airplanes, and he remembered Crosson from San Diego. Joe was well qualified, but oblivious to the primitive flying conditions that awaited him. The development of aviation in the Territory of Alaska was easily ten years behind the rest of the country.

Flying developed at different paces in each region of Alaska because of unique terrain, weather, and transportation needs. Southeast and Southcentral Alaska already enjoyed relatively adequate access via ocean transportation. Temperatures were moderate in those regions compared with Interior Alaska and the Arctic, but fog and storms made flying difficult for weeks at a time.

Arctic Alaska, sparsely populated and with little economic activity

March 16, 1926
Robert Goddard launches the first liquid-fueled rocket, at Auburn Massachusetts, where it travels 184 feet.

◄ *An unusual Fokker F.III sat unused in Fairbanks when Joe arrived. He was the only pilot other than Noel Wien to fly the craft, in which the pilot sat in the open, next to the motor, while the passengers rode in an enclosed cabin.*

to demand increased transportation, was slow to take advantage of
aviation. Flying in the Southeast, Southcentral, and the Arctic didn't
take hold until after its development in the Interior.

In 1926, Interior Alaska needed aviation and was embracing the new technology. At the time, transportation options were few. Shallow-draft stern-wheelers on larger rivers and small boats on the others provided passage in the summer. The Alaska Railroad connected the Interior to Seward on the southern coast, and some of the gold camps were served by narrow-gauge railroad. A horse-drawn stage was the most reliable transportation between Fairbanks and another coastal town, Valdez, but a businessman named Bobby Sheldon was taking passengers on the same route in his "auto-stage." Other than these, getting around meant walking along the trail system or venturing cross-country. Wider trails were called wagon roads, but most were not good enough for motorized vehicles. In winter, dog teams delivered freight and passengers around the region, but travel was slow and hazardous.

A resurgent interest in gold mining in Alaska's Interior after World War I made it a growing industry that could support new modes of transportation. The population center of Fairbanks, the largest city in the Territory, was a likely location for the airplane to appear.

The story of flying in Alaska began in 1913, about the time Joe and Marvel Crosson were setting their sights on the sky at the fairground in Sterling, Colorado. The first plane came to Alaska to fly an exhibition during the summer of 1913. An enterprising group of businessmen brought up a biplane designed, built, and owned by J. V. and Lily Martin.

Just getting the plane to Alaska involved an epic journey. The plane was crated in Seattle and loaded on a steamship for a ride to Skagway. Next it was loaded on the White Pass and Yukon Railroad for a trip to Whitehorse, Yukon Territory, where it was transferred to a paddle wheeler for a journey down the Yukon and up the Tanana and Chena Rivers. Chugging up the river into Fairbanks, the paddle wheeler delivered its payload. The crates were unloaded, and the plane was reassembled at the ballpark.

The businessmen who bankrolled the venture planned to charge a hefty admission to view the modern marvel in action. Unfortunately for them, it quickly became apparent there was no pressing reason to pay admission. At the time of the big show, local residents climbed on top of their woodpiles and up on their roofs to watch the plane and

The story of flying in Alaska began in 1913, about the time Joe and Marvel Crosson were setting their sights on the sky at the fairground in Sterling, Colorado.

◄ *Shortly after coming to Alaska, Joe Crosson was again at the controls of a rebuilt Jenny. Joe test-flew the Fairbanks Airplane Corporation's craft in April 1926 and regularly used it to instruct students.*

▲ Joe spent many days repairing planes in the Fairbanks Airplane Corporation hangar at Rickert's Field—originally part of Paul Rickert's farm.

save the price of admission. Although the show wasn't a financial success, it planted the aviation seed in the minds of people in Fairbanks. Following the show, the plane was recrated for another riverboat journey, down the Chena and Tanana Rivers to the mouth of the Yukon for a steamship ride back to Seattle.

The next airplanes didn't fly in Alaska until 1920, the same year the Crossons moved to San Diego. The flights were the brainchild of Brigadier General Billy Mitchell and were made by U.S. Army pilots. Mitchell recognized that the Territory was strategically located for long-range aviation to Europe and Asia. He also saw that Alaska could play a vital role in protecting the United States from invasion.

In an attempt to draw attention to the faraway Territory and obtain continued funding for aviation, Mitchell organized a flight of four U.S. Army deHavilland biplanes from New York to Nome and back. The flight of what was called the Black Wolf Squadron included stops at Fairbanks in both directions. Enthusiastic crowds met the squadron all along the route. The flights showed that airplanes could be used dependably for cross-country operations in Alaska. Enthusiasm grew for flying in the Territory.

About the time Joe and Marvel were learning to fly in 1921, Clarence Prest was attempting to become the first pilot to fly from Mexico to Siberia through Alaska. On his first effort, Prest's airplane was destroyed in a windstorm at Prince Rupert, British Columbia.

Prest began a second attempt to fly to Siberia in May 1922. This time he started in New York and flew to Seattle. Prest then shipped his plane to Juneau and flew from there to Eagle on the Yukon River. He left Eagle for the two-hundred-mile flight to Fairbanks, but his engine failed and he was forced to land on a gravel bar. Searchers from Eagle found Prest in good health. Prest's damaged plane was left at the site, but he salvaged some parts and traveled to Fairbanks on boats and the railroad.

Prest was greeted by citizens eager to learn more about aviation. Among them was Ben Eielson, a high school teacher and former pilot in the Army Air Service. Local businessmen had the financing necessary to back an aviation venture, and Eielson was an able and willing pilot. Although Prest had failed in his attempt to reach Siberia, his presence encouraged the birth of an aviation industry in Alaska.

In early 1923 the Farthest-North Airplane Company was founded by R. C. Wood of the First National Bank of Fairbanks, W. F. Thompson of the *Fairbanks Daily News-Miner*, and Ben Eielson. It was a bold move for a town of fewer than two thousand people. A surplus JN-4D Jenny was shipped to Fairbanks in pieces, reassembled at the ballpark, and soon took to the skies over town. Eielson spent the summer of 1923 pioneering air routes to Interior Alaska towns and mining camps. Trips that had taken days or weeks on the ground during previous summers were accomplished in mere hours by air.

In early 1924, when Joe and Marvel were taking passengers for rides in San Diego, Eielson flew the first experimental air mail contracts sponsored by the U.S. Post Office. The flights enjoyed some success and encouraged even more entrepreneurs in Fairbanks to enter

About the time Joe and Marvel were learning to fly in 1921, Clarence Prest was attempting to become the first pilot to fly from Mexico to Siberia through Alaska. On his first effort, Prest's airplane was destroyed in a windstorm at Prince Rupert, British Columbia.

When the cheerful young Joe Crosson stepped off the Alaska Railroad train into the frigid air of Fairbanks on March 2, 1926, his family home in San Diego seemed a million miles away.

the flying business. Following the 1924 flying season Eielson left Alaska, but he would be back.

A second flying company in Fairbanks was started during 1924. The Alaska Aerial Transportation Company was formed by James Rodebaugh, a conductor for the Alaska Railroad. He had amassed a considerable stake by trading furs along the rail line and was eager to join in the flying business. Rodebaugh headed outside in search of planes and pilots to get his venture off the ground.

Rodebaugh bought two Standard J-1's in Minnesota during the spring of 1924, shipped them to Fairbanks, and hired two pilots to fly them. One left after the first season. The other, Noel Wien, devoted his life to developing aviation in the Territory.

At the end of the flying season, negotiations to merge the two companies began. In early 1925, the Alaska Aerial Transportation Company and the Farthest-North Airplane Company became the Fairbanks Airplane Corporation, and many enthusiastic citizens bought shares in the new business.

Rodebaugh managed the merged operation. Wien was now the only permanent pilot in the region, and more talent was needed. This time Rodebaugh hired a flight instructor who had given him lessons in San Diego. Within weeks A. A. Bennett was flying the vast, uncharted skies of Alaska.

As the 1925 flying season drew to an end, Wien departed the Territory. Like Eielson he would return to leave his mark on flying in Alaska. In the meantime, the Fairbanks Airplane Corporation was again down to one pilot. While A. A. Bennett was tackling some of the first serious winter flying in Alaska, another pilot was badly needed, and again the company hired a man from San Diego. That man was Joe Crosson.

~

WHEN THE CHEERFUL young Joe Crosson stepped off the Alaska Railroad train into the frigid air of Fairbanks on March 2, 1926, his family home in San Diego seemed a million miles away. He had left the

midwinter 70-degree temperatures of Southern California for the
snowy, subzero weather of Fairbanks. He missed his family. Here he
was not big brother to Zelma, little brother to Marvel, nor favored son
of Elizabeth and Esler Crosson. He was simply a twenty-three-year-old
man, unproven, and on his own for the first time. A pilot who was
highly skilled, mechanically capable, quick-witted, intelligent, not
easily discouraged, and extremely lucky could prosper if he came to
Alaska in those days. Joe Crosson was one of the few who fully fit
the bill.

When the temperature dipped below 10 degrees Fahrenheit, pilots had to drain the oil following each flight and take it indoors. Buckets of motor oil were left near woodstoves each night to keep them warm and the warm oil was poured back into the crankcase.

As community development goes, Fairbanks was a mere infant in
1926. The gold mining town, founded in 1901, was only two years
older than the young pilot. But Fairbanks was destined to become a
transportation hub. It was situated at the end of the recently completed
Alaska Railroad and at the upriver terminus for paddle-wheel freight
on the Tanana and Chena Rivers—a perfect location for the expanding
flying industry in Interior Alaska. Rich, gold-bearing deposits in the
region guaranteed a constant demand for year-round transportation,
and the airplane was rapidly becoming a preferred method of travel.

Airplanes flew from a former farm field at the outskirts of
Fairbanks. By any standard, flying from Rickert's Field was primitive,
not a bit like the California airfields Joe was used to. There was one dirt
landing strip, one small hangar, and one other local pilot, Bennett. The
hodgepodge fleet of airplanes was composed of two Standards, a Jenny,
and one Fokker F.III.

The planes were powered by early-model liquid-cooled motors
that were far from reliable, especially in the Alaskan cold. When the
temperature dipped below 10 degrees Fahrenheit, pilots had to drain
the oil following each flight and take it indoors so it wouldn't congeal
in the engine. Buckets of motor oil were left near woodstoves each
night to keep them warm. Before a flight, engines were warmed with a
plumber's torch under a canvas tarp and the warm oil was poured back
into the crankcase.

After these preparations, pilots hand-propped the engines to start
them. If the plane didn't start within a few minutes, the oil had to be
drained again and both oil and motor reheated for another try.

Bennett was not about to let the newcomer jump in and pilot one of the only flyable planes in Alaska. Despite freezing temperatures, Crosson longed to fly. But for the time being he was stuck in the hangar.

Cooling systems were susceptible to leaks or freezing, causing motors to overheat during the colder months. The short winter days (less than four hours of daylight in midwinter), lack of runways, and absence of good maps added to the challenges.

When Crosson reported to the Fairbanks Airplane Corporation hangar, the company fleet was in various stages of repair. The odd, cumbersome-looking Fokker F.III sat unused and flew only a couple more times before being retired. The Standard J-1's remained airworthy, and one sported a recent addition, a locally designed and as yet untested enclosed cabin to protect passengers from the weather. The company's original Jenny sat disassembled in the hangar.

The chief, and only other, company pilot, A. A. Bennett, relegated Crosson to mechanic duties. Like Crosson, Bennett was known for both his piloting ability and mechanical skills. Unlike Crosson, however he was not known for his pleasant demeanor. Bennett was not about to let the newcomer jump in and pilot one of the only flyable planes in Alaska. He expected the new man to prove himself in the hangar, rebuilding airplanes, before taking to the sky. Despite freezing temperatures, Crosson longed to fly. But for the time being he was stuck in the hangar.

To make his grounding even worse, Fairbanks was alive with aviation activity. Three aerial expeditions were attempting a polar flight in 1926. Two were based in Spitsbergen, Norway: Admiral Richard Byrd planned to fly a Ford Tri-Motor over the North Pole, while Roald Amundsen anticipated crossing the pole in a dirigible.

The third expedition was headquartered in Fairbanks. Led by Captain Hubert Wilkins, the Detroit Arctic Expedition was the first of his three attempts to fly across the top of the world. Wilkins brought his chief pilot Ben Eielson, his crew, and two huge Fokker airplanes to Fairbanks to mount the challenge.

Flying activity and excitement surrounding the expedition was nearly unbearable for a young pilot still confined to hangar duty. Crosson was twenty-three and certainly not immune to the impatience of youth. After three long weeks on the ground, he could wait no longer. The Standard with the homebuilt cabin had not been flown since it was modified. On March 20, when A. A. Bennett (who had designed and built the cabin) was out flying, Crosson took the plane up for a test flight.

The test could have been a disaster. Joe was rusty after more than a month without flying, plus he had never flown in below-freezing temperatures. Only fifteen minutes into the flight the engine cut out, but the skilled young pilot avoided disaster and glided safely back to the field. His logbook noted the event with a simple entry of "engine failure." In his mind the event may have been minor, but that was not the case with Chief Pilot Bennett. He was agitated by the brash move, minced no words in telling Crosson so, grounded him once more, and again limited his duties to mechanics. Joe wasn't allowed back in the cockpit for nearly a month.

Finally, by mid-April 1926, Crosson was regularly in the air in the Standards. He also reassembled the Jenny and taught flying lessons in it. His early students included Andy Hufford, who was a mechanic for Hubert Wilkins, and Noel Wien's brother Ralph.

Only fifteen minutes into the flight the engine cut out, but the skilled young pilot avoided disaster and glided safely back to the field. His logbook noted the event with a simple entry of "engine failure."

Joe in Teller, Alaska

3

RACE FROM THE COAST

Fairbanks, May 1926. Crosson watched the activities of Hubert Wilkins and Ben Eielson and the excitement that accompanied their attempt to fly across the top of the world in 1926 with much interest. As part of their effort, Wilkins and Eielson pioneered the air route to Barrow, Alaska's farthest-north community, but were then held there by bad weather.

As the men waited out a blizzard at Point Barrow, the other aerial explorers heading for the North Pole at the same time met with success. Admiral Richard Byrd flew his Ford Tri-Motor to the pole and returned to Spitsbergen, Norway, on May 9. Roald Amundsen and his crew boarded the dirigible *Norge* in Spitsbergen on May 11, successfully crossed the North Pole, and touched down at the village of Teller, Alaska, on May 13.

May 11 found Crosson in the tiny mining community of Flat, Alaska, making a series of flights that took him to McGrath and eventually home to Fairbanks. He was now the sole pilot for Fairbanks Airplane Corporation since his former bosses, A. A. Bennett and Jimmy Rodebaugh, had formed their own company with newer planes shipped into Alaska. Joe was unaware of what had taken place that day at the top of the world, nor did he know that he would soon be involved in the story.

April 16, 1926

The U.S. Department of Agriculture purchases its first crop-dusting plane.

◄ *Joe Crosson couldn't resist posing in Teller after becoming the first pilot to reach the Seward Peninsula to retrieve pictures of the dirigible Norge.*

That same morning the dirigible *Norge* was pulled from its berth on Spitsbergen Island, north of Norway in the Arctic Ocean, and readied for its historic flight. The ground crew maneuvered the huge craft with guide ropes as the flight crew—Norwegian Roald Amundsen, American Lincoln Ellsworth, Italian Umberto Nobile, and thirteen others—made final preparations. The expedition was conceived by Amundsen. The airship was designed and built by Nobile and largely financed by the Aero Club of Norway and the industrialist father of Lincoln Ellsworth.

The *Norge* was a semi-rigid dirigible 348 feet long. The ship was lifted by internal gas bags filled with highly volatile hydrogen and powered by three 230-horsepower engines mounted on the exterior. In the front of the ship the main cabin housed flight controls. Each engine was enclosed in a "boat," a frame that allowed crew members to climb in and service the engines from the girderlike skeleton that gave the craft its shape.

Amundsen's crew was somewhat subdued by Admiral Byrd's successful flight over the pole just two days earlier. But, as Amundsen emphasized, the goal of his expedition was scientific, in pursuit of uncharted land between the continents. Being the first to reach the North Pole by air had been only a secondary goal. Shortly before ten o'clock on the morning of May 11, 1926, the *Norge* was launched.

The dirigible's flight lasted nearly seventy-one hours and was a huge triumph in arctic aviation. As the *Norge* passed over the North Pole, the aviators dropped flags of Norway, Italy, and the United States. No new land was discovered as the *Norge* continued on to Alaska, but the flight was not without event. Ice built up in layers on the huge propellers. Jagged shards of ice were flung through the ship's outer skin and nearly punctured the gas bags, which would have meant certain disaster. The dirigible was at the mercy of the stiff arctic wind, and at times the crew had little or no control over its direction. Bad weather prevented the *Norge* from landing at Nome, so the crew aimed for Teller.

Nome was awaiting the triumphant arrival, and residents had planned a huge reception. Teller, on the other hand, was a small town about eighty miles up the western coast. People in the town were only

Landing at Ten...

The Norge after Landing, Teller, Alaska

▲ Joe stands next to hydrogen gas cylinders on the ice at Teller. The lighter-than-air but highly flammable gas allowed the Norge to fly.

mildly aware of the historic flight. Instead of a large, formal welcoming ceremony, only a few surprised Eskimos and reindeer herders greeted the international travelers.

The flight of the dirigible was a great success, and to this day no airship has repeated the feat. The world demanded to see images of this first transpolar crossing. Pathé News Service hired Joe Crosson to deliver newsreel film of the event from Teller to Fairbanks. At the same time, a competing company, International News Reel, hired A. A. Bennett to fly film from the *Norge*. At least one newspaper referred to these film delivery flights as a race.

Getting pictures from this remote region of Alaska to the rest of the world meant someone had to fly a photographer to Teller, then fly the film out of Teller so it could be shipped to the continental United States. The race focused attention on the veteran Alaskan pilot Bennett and on newcomer Joe Crosson, who had never before flown to Alaska's western coast.

Pathé News wanted Crosson to fly the film from Teller to the Alaska Railroad in Fairbanks. Crosson and one of his student pilots, Andy Hufford, left Fairbanks in a Standard J-1 late in the afternoon of May 15 and spent the night in Ruby. The next morning they flew to Nome, picked up a cameraman, and continued on to Teller.

A. A. Bennett was flying a Waco for International News Reel, accompanied by mechanic Ed Young. They left Fairbanks early on the morning of May 16 and picked up their photographer in Nome on the way to Teller.

After the photographers took pictures of the dismantled *Norge*, both Crosson and Bennett flew their crews back to Nome to spend the night. Though both planes left Nome for Fairbanks at the same time on May 17, the Waco was faster, helping Bennett and Young reach Fairbanks fifteen minutes ahead of Crosson and Hufford. The film, however, was still thousands of miles from Seattle and the awaiting audiences.

From Fairbanks, the International News Reel film was flown to Skagway in Southeast Alaska, shipped to British Columbia, then flown to Seattle on May 27. The Pathé film traveled first on the Alaska Railroad from Fairbanks and then on a steamship to Seattle. It arrived in Seattle on May 28, a full fifteen days after the *Norge* had landed at Teller.

The race made headlines in Alaska's newspapers. After flying for only two months in Alaska, Crosson was becoming well known in the Territory and was even gaining recognition in the rest of the country. The flights had proven his competence as a bush pilot, and he was learning the land and its idiosyncrasies.

▼ *Joe Crosson flew to Teller shortly after the Norge landed, in this Standard J-1 with enclosed passenger cabin. Later in 1926, Joe narrowly avoided death when the craft burst into flame in flight.*

Waco nosed over

4
CHEATING DEATH

Summer 1926. During June and July following the 1926 *Norge* "film race," Joe Crosson continued his education in the business of flying in Alaska through on-the-job training—the only school available for young pilots in the Territory. New flights took him from Fairbanks throughout Interior Alaska: north to Wiseman in the foothills of the rugged Brooks Range, northwest to the mining town of Livengood, southwest to Lake Minchumina, and west to Ruby. Between flights, he taught a group of eager students how to fly.

During the year Crosson became the first pilot to fly to the trading post of Bettles on the Koyukuk River to the north, and the first to land on a Kuskokwim River bar at the Yupik Eskimo village of Bethel, five hundred miles southwest of Fairbanks. Slowly and methodically, he helped to lengthen the distance airplanes could travel in Alaska. But it wasn't easy.

Pilots of open-cockpit planes endured bone-chilling wind in winter, sunburned faces in summer, and deafening noise year-round. Runways were few and far between, with no accurate maps to locate them. Props and landing gear on the frail craft often broke. Motors were notoriously undependable, regularly offering up a series of close calls for pilots.

July 2, 1926
The first known reforestation by airplane is carried out in Hawaii.

◄ *Minor mishaps were a typical hazard of the job for early pilots in Alaska. Soft snow, short fields, and rough surfaces caused many planes to nose over, often damaging propellers and motors.*

► *Gold miners Fannie and Joe Quigley became good friends with Joe Crosson—despite the fact Crosson was at the controls when Quigley was injured in a landing mishap.*

Crosson developed a reputation for his abilities in all sorts of difficult situations, and for his good humor. Bob Gleason, who worked with Joe throughout the 1930s, knew the pilot and his skills well. According to Gleason, Joe was "the kind of guy who didn't mind trouble. He would get through any way he could. He was extremely able."

By the end of 1926, Crosson's logbook carried several simple entries reflecting his skill, luck, and the potential for disaster that accompanied almost every flight: "Test hop after engine work." "Test hop (more troubles)." "Test after repair of oil tank." "150 miles over fog." "Snow storm (broke con rod)." "Bad fog (Fearless Joe)."

Despite the understated entries, several flights mentioned in the logbook were notable, including one that resulted in the only passenger ever injured while in Crosson's care. He recorded the event simply as, "to Nenana, Moose Creek nosed over." There is more to the story.

At the end of July, pioneer miner Joe Quigley asked Crosson to fly him to a runway at his mine in the Kantishna mining district, near Mount McKinley. All Fairbanks Airplane Corporation planes were being repaired at the time, so Crosson was temporarily flying for the Bennett-Rodebaugh Company in its new Waco. Accompanied by fellow pilot Ed Young, the three men made the flight from Fairbanks with no problems. But arriving at Quigley's mine, Crosson looked out his windshield with concern. The so-called runway was nowhere near long enough for a plane. Joe had just learned the hard way that miners and pilots had different ideas about where a plane could land. Joe said later, with a laugh, that miners would say they had a fine field, but "an eagle couldn't even land there."

After looking over the terrain, Crosson turned the Waco and set up a pattern to land on a nearby gravel bar in Moose Creek near Kantishna. He recalled the landing:

"We sailed over a bunch of stumps and hit. The gravel was hard as pavement. I no more touched than I saw I was going to run in the river, so I poured on the coal. But the Waco slowed up and rapidly ended up in the water, stuck on its nose just slightly upside down at a forty-five degree angle—in those days a favorite position."

Joe had just learned the hard way that miners and pilots had different ideas about where a plane could land. Joe said later, with a laugh, that miners would say they had a fine field, but "an eagle couldn't even land there."

▲ *Joe Crosson flew this Waco aircraft to the Kantishna mining district in July 1926 to take Joe Quigley back to his gold mine. During the landing, the plane nosed over on a gravel bar. Quigley's gashed nose was the only injury ever sustained by any passenger who flew with Crosson.*

Crosson and Young were unscathed, but Quigley and the Waco were not. On impact, Joe Quigley sustained a nasty gash on the nose that was bleeding profusely. His wife, Fannie, was a seasoned miner, known for her hard work, salty language, and frontier can-do attitude. Fannie watched the landing and quickly sized up the situation. After a terse remark to Crosson—"Christ, what are you trying to do, kill my man?"—she went to work. Using a crude medical kit she took on the task of sewing up her husband's injured nose. Joe Crosson remembered it all:

"First she tried a baseball stitch, but she couldn't get the skin to pull even, so she finally decided to sew it up just straight. Then by golly she poured on a lot of iodine. Poor Joe was in torture. His nose looked like a pan of hamburger but it healed okay."

~

JOE QUIGLEY'S ORDEAL was over, but the flyers still had an airplane in the river. They dragged the Waco out and turned it right side up. It was in no shape to fly. Tips of the metal propeller were bent and the crankcase was broken. The aviators were 150 miles from Fairbanks with no radio or means to get a message out.

After the Waco failed to return to Fairbanks for two days, the boss flew to Moose Creek to check out the situation. A. A. Bennett scoured the hills and valleys looking for the plane. He finally spotted it on the Moose Creek bar. Since he could see only minor damage, he concluded the stranded pair was probably on the trail walking out. He was right. At the time Crosson and Young were two days into one of the most miserable weeks of their lives.

Fannie had given them clear directions on the best way to get to Savage River in Mount McKinley National Park, where they could pick up the park road to the Alaska Railroad. But shortly after leaving her place they met an old prospector who was heading for the same destination. He convinced the aviators to take a shortcut with him that could shave miles and days off their journey. The shortcut turned out to be eighty-five miles along swampy trails, through mud holes, and across huge fields of tussocks, the mounds of grass that grow in swamps. Trying to step on top of the tussocks caused the men to twist their ankles and fall, but stepping over and around the two-foot-tall lumps required them to walk through the puddles between the tussocks and resulted in wet feet and aching legs. Blisters erupted on their feet. Branches slapped them in the face. Mosquitoes and biting flies swarmed over them by the millions.

To make things worse, the prospector couldn't keep up under the weight of his pack, so Crosson and Young took turns carrying the pack along with their own gear. They were hot and sweaty during the day, but taking off their jackets only made them more vulnerable to insects. At night they shivered near the campfire, hoping the smoke would keep the bugs away, dreading the next day's journey, and wishing they had never met the prospector.

The shortcut turned out to be eighty-five miles along swampy trails, through mud holes, and across huge fields of tussocks. Blisters erupted on their feet. Branches slapped them in the face. Mosquitoes and biting flies swarmed over them by the millions.

▲ *Residents of McGrath go to the rescue of Joe Crosson and his two passengers in the Kuskokwim River. The three men were stranded after the motor failed in Joe's Super Swallow during takeoff November 9, 1926, and he crash-landed in the river. Rescuers rowed out to the plane between floating chunks of ice.*

At the Savage River, they arrived at a camp that had been set up for tourists, and the exhausted men fell asleep in tents. The next morning, Crosson and Young watched as the old prospector paraded in front of the tourists and their cameras, wearing his pack and bragging about how he had just hiked in from the bush.

The flyers caught a ride to the nearby Alaska Railroad station and hopped the train back to Fairbanks. Within days Crosson was test-flying another Bennett-Rodebaugh plane, one that was fresh out of the repair shop.

Crosson returned to Joe Quigley's place and the ailing Waco the following week, in early August, with George King, another skilled mechanic. This time he landed safely on a larger gravel bar several miles away. It took a day to ferry their heavy tools and parts to the damaged plane, where the two men spent several days replacing or

repairing the broken parts of the Waco—more than a hundred miles from the nearest hangar or shop. In mid-August, Crosson flew the Waco off the bar on Moose Creek for an uneventful trip back to Fairbanks.

~

BY THE TIME Joe retrieved the Waco, the Fairbanks Airplane Corporation's new plane, a Super Swallow, had arrived. Setting a safety record for the era, Joe flew for more than two months with no major problems, but new challenges awaited.

Crosson's November 9 entry states, "motor failure - landed in the Kuskokwim River." The notation glosses over another arduous adventure. Crosson had spent a couple of days based in McGrath, flying in and out of other gold camps in the region. On November 9, he loaded two

▲ *McGrath residents prepare to pull Crosson's Super Swallow from the icy Kuskokwim. The plane was badly damaged when it was pulled from the river, but gold being transported by two miners was retrieved.*

"We heaved. The horses heaved. Suddenly the plane hopped up on the bank. Her tail was off. Her wings were all in pieces. All that was left of our new Swallow was the motor."

miners and their year-end cargo of gold into the new Super Swallow. Immediately after takeoff from the Kuskokwim River gravel bar that served as a runway, the engine quit. Crosson leveled the plane and crash-landed in the river. The plane came to rest upright on a sand bar in about four feet of nearly freezing water, with no one injured.

The river was running with large chunks of ice. If Crosson and the two miners got out of the plane and tried to cross the river, they would be swept downstream to a certain death. Residents of McGrath launched a small boat and rowed out to rescue the men, but the current and ice made maneuvering difficult. Crosson and his passengers were soaked, and even by standing on the seats were not able to get completely out of the icy water. They shivered for nearly an hour before the boat arrived and picked them up. Back on shore, the three men were rushed inside and warmed. After they were warm and dry, they hatched a plan to retrieve the stranded Super Swallow and its cargo (more than $35,000 worth of gold!).

The local citizens again launched their boat and rowed out through the treacherous waters to the disabled plane. This time they attached ropes to the plane. They hitched the ropes to a team of horses on the river bank, and the horses, with the help of the pilot and the miners, dragged the plane through the river and out of the water. Crosson later wrote: "We heaved. The horses heaved. Suddenly the plane hopped up on the bank. Her tail was off. Her wings were all in pieces. All that was left of our new Swallow was the motor."

But the travelers were safe and the gold was retrieved. Parts of the Super Swallow were freighted back to Fairbanks. It is a tribute to the resourcefulness of early aviators that the plane was rebuilt and flew again early the next year.

∼

THE LOSS OF the Super Swallow for the season was a severe blow to the Fairbanks Airplane Corporation. The only other plane the company owned that was even close to being in flying condition was the cabined Standard J-1 that Crosson had first flown when he arrived in Alaska.

But that plane was resting on a gravel bar on the Toklat River, a hundred miles from Fairbanks, where Crosson had left it after yet another engine failure and harrowing overland trek in October.

Airplanes were badly needed in McGrath to carry passengers, following several days of thick fog that had prevented air travel. With no other craft available, someone had to go to the Toklat River to get the Standard back in the air.

On November 13, just four days after the accident with the Super Swallow, Crosson, mechanic Ernie Franzen, and a load of tools and parts were flown out to the Toklat River by Ed Young and A. A. Bennett. Crosson and Franzen intended to repair the Standard and fly it to McGrath to pick up passengers before returning to Fairbanks.

Winter begins in earnest in November in Interior Alaska. Rivers were frozen and snow covered the ground. The days were short. Daytime temperatures climbed only into the teens and dropped well below zero at night. Crosson and Franzen had a formidable task ahead of them just battling the weather to stay warm, let alone repairing an airplane engine in the middle of nowhere.

Cold robbed them of energy. They built and fueled a huge bonfire during the day. They did as much of the work as they could wearing huge fur mitts, but needed bare fingers for the finer adjustments. When their fingers became clumsy and numb with cold, they moved closer to the fire to warm up, then kept at it. The fire also warmed the motor parts and oil, and heated the frozen ground. At night they brushed away the coals and slept in their bedrolls on the warm spot.

For three days Franzen and Crosson labored on the Standard's motor during the few short hours of daylight and by firelight. The plane's elevators had been left in tatters by wind and also had to be repaired. But by November 15 they were back in the air.

They flew to a lake near Diamond on the Kantishna River and spent another frigid night. Only after the oil was drained and the airplane secured could they build a warming fire for themselves and finally get some sleep. In the morning they warmed the oil over the campfire and heated the motor before starting it and flying on to Lake Minchumina.

Crosson and Franzen had a formidable task ahead of them just battling the weather to stay warm, let alone repairing an airplane engine in the middle of nowhere.

He smelled smoke and then saw flames. It was every pilot's worst nightmare: the engine was on fire, and they were fifteen hundred feet in the air.

The warm roadhouse in Minchumina was a welcome change from the past few cold nights. The next morning Crosson and Franzen again warmed the oil and motor, fired up the engine, and took off for McGrath. They smiled as they cruised along. It appeared the Fairbanks Airplane Corporation was back in business.

About fifty miles short of McGrath, Crosson's heart nearly stopped. He smelled smoke and then saw flames. It was every pilot's worst nightmare: the engine was on fire, and they were fifteen hundred feet in the air. He had to land immediately. He sideslipped to lose altitude and headed for a frozen lake as the flames started to eat into the fuselage. Coughing and eyes watering from the smoke, Franzen shielded Crosson from the flames with a piece of burlap while he landed the plane. The Standard came to a stop, and Crosson and Franzen tumbled out of the burning cabin into the frozen air and watched as fire consumed the old bird. They had narrowly escaped death and were not injured, but that's where the good news stopped. They were 250 air miles from home, stranded in the Alaska wilderness in winter.

The two men trudged eight miles through the snow to the roadhouse at Berry's Landing by nightfall. From there, they planned to hike the dogsled trails to McGrath the following day to wire for Bennett or Ed Young to fly out and pick them up. To their dismay, they found Bennett at Berry's Landing, stranded with a broken propeller on his plane.

The next day Crosson and Franzen walked west to McGrath and the radio link to Fairbanks. Getting picked up by Young was their best bet to get back home in a reasonable time. However, in McGrath they learned that Young was stranded near Telida, about one hundred miles east of McGrath, with engine trouble. In a remarkable twist of fate, all three of the pilots flying in Interior Alaska were down in the same region at the same time.

A. A. Bennett received a new propeller by dog team by the end of the month and eventually flew out of Berry's Landing. Young was fortunate enough to catch a ride with a dog team and made it to the train in Nenana within six days.

Crosson and Franzen were not so lucky. More than two hundred miles of dogsled trails lay between them and the train. They started walking, hoping that a dog team would happen along and offer them a ride, but none did.

Temperatures dropped to minus 40 degrees Fahrenheit. The men wore heavy fur flying suits, but the days still were incredibly cold, long, and exhausting. For eleven days they walked, rested, built warming fires, and then walked some more. When they could find no roadhouse nearby, they again heated the ground with a fire and slept in the burned area. After a grueling two hundred miles on foot in bitter cold, they reached Nenana, weak from fatigue. They were able to catch the train back to Fairbanks.

In his logbook, Joe told the story this way: "Plane burned up—had to walk back to Fairbanks."

After a grueling two hundred miles on foot in bitter cold, they reached Nenana, weak from fatigue.

Hubert Wilson and Joe

5

ALONE IN THE ARCTIC

Winter 1927. Winter days are long, dark, and cold in Interior Alaska. At the depths of winter the sun rises just before noon and sets after illuminating the land for a scant few hours, often taking a toll on the human psyche. The amount of work Crosson faced in the hangar helped his first winter in Alaska pass quickly.

The forced landing in the Kuskokwim River at McGrath had left the Super Swallow in tatters. The plane returned in pieces by boat and rail and had to be rebuilt. In spite of damage to the wings, landing gear, and fuselage, Crosson and the other mechanics had the plane back in top condition on skis, complete with a new propeller, by early March of 1927. He was once again flying it over uncharted regions of Alaska long before spring.

Even in winter, some ambitious students wanted to learn to fly. It took courage to put on enough layers of wool and fur to sit in an open-cockpit plane, with prop wash bringing the wind chill factor to 100 degrees below zero. When weather allowed and students were tough enough, Crosson was happy to teach them. His primary student that winter was local miner George King. King's lessons were the only flights Crosson logged during January and February 1927.

In addition, he replaced the engine on the Jenny. The OX-5 motor

April 4, 1927

Colonial Air Transport establishes scheduled passenger service between New York and Boston.

◄ *Joe Crosson and explorer Hubert Wilkins exchange remarks. Wilkins gained great respect for the young pilot following Joe's daring flight to Barrow in 1927 in support of a Wilkins expedition. Because of the flight, Wilkins chose Joe as a pilot for his 1928 Antarctic expedition.*

It took courage to put on enough layers of wool and fur to sit in an open-cockpit plane, with prop wash bringing the wind chill factor to 100 degrees below zero.

on the aging bird had become undependable and was replaced with a new Hisso.

Joe Crosson had been in Alaska for only one year. At twenty-four years old, he was one of the most experienced members of an elite group—respected pilots in Alaska. His contemporaries included Ben Eielson, Noel Wien, Ed Young, and A. A. Bennett. Each had been the first in the air in different corners of the Alaska sky, and each had survived harrowing experiences. Although he was the "new kid on the block," Joe's ability soon led him on a new adventure well above the Arctic Circle.

~

HUBERT WILKINS returned to Fairbanks during February 1927 in a second attempt to fly in the high Arctic above the North American continent. The air of excitement Wilkins brought to Fairbanks the previous winter was renewed. The Australian explorer planned to land on the ice pack in the far north and take soundings to determine the depth of water under the ice. If the water was shallow, indicating land may be present, he would continue north. If the water was deep, indicating no land was present, he would return to Barrow.

Wilkins reenlisted pilots Ben Eielson and Alger Graham from the previous year's flights and added experienced Alaskan pilot Noel Wien to his crew. Parts of two Fokker airplanes used during the last attempt were combined to build one functional aircraft, and two new Stinson Detroiter biplanes rounded out the fleet. Wilkins now had state-of-the-art equipment and two of the most experienced pilots in Alaska. It looked as if this time, his effort would meet with success. The venture was named the *Detroit News*-Wilkins Arctic Expedition in recognition of its sponsoring newspaper.

Noel Wien was given the controls of one Stinson, Alger Graham handled the controls of the other, and Ben Eielson flew the big Fokker. Winterizing and outfitting the three planes took weeks. Meanwhile, Joe Crosson was busy in Interior Alaska, flying as far as Nome, the coastal mining town on the Seward Peninsula.

The ski-equipped planes of the Wilkins expedition were started and taxied out to the end of the landing strip in Fairbanks on March 24. The smaller Stinson Detroiter biplanes had no trouble maneuvering as they readied for takeoff, but the huge lumbering Fokker was another story. While turning around, one of the skis caught in a rut and the gear collapsed, and the Fokker was out of commission.

Wilkins faced a predicament. His backers expected the expedition to continue, but he was without one third of his air fleet and could haul less than two-thirds of the gear he'd planned to take. Wilkins hurriedly changed his plans.

Wien was released from service and Eielson took the controls of the Stinson. Graham remained in the other Stinson. The crew reevaluated how much gear and how many men they could carry. Wilkins decided to leave one mechanic behind and also to fill the extra seat (which had been allocated to a *Detroit News* reporter) with gear. Without the Fokker, this arrangement offered the best chance at success. It also presented another problem.

Since the expedition was sponsored by the *Detroit News*, Wilkins desperately needed to get its reporter, A. M. Smith, to Barrow to witness the arctic flights. Wilkins turned to the Fairbanks Airplane Corporation, which offered an unbeatable combination: a flyable airplane and an experienced pilot.

~

Joe Crosson got notice of the flight with little warning and readily agreed to it. He had been flying the Super Swallow on commercial hops for a week and knew how the plane performed. The biplane could only fly just over four hours on one tank of gas. Because of this short range, he would need to stop at the small mining community of Wiseman, about two and a half hours north of Fairbanks, to refuel before he reached the Brooks Range and uncharted territory on the way to Barrow.

Navigation was yet another challenge. When Crosson agreed to make the flight, Eielson and Wilkins were the only people who had ever flown to the northern tip of Alaska. No accurate map showed the

Barrow was 330 miles to the north. His magnetic compass was marginal help at best, because the needle pointed between 25 and 30 degrees east of true north—toward the magnetic north pole in Canada, which is hundreds of miles south of the true North Pole.

FAIRBANKS AIRPLANE CORPORATION.
25 MARCH 1927

FIRST COMMERCIAL FLIGHT TO POINT BARROW.
FIRST AIR FLIGHT BARROW-KOTZEBUE-RUBY.
· SWALLOW· WRIGHT E.

	Distance Miles	Flying Time Hrs. Min
Fairbanks to Wiseman	225	2-25
Wiseman to Pt. Barrow	330	4-35
Pt Barrow to Cape Sabin	280	
Cape Sabine to Cape Thompson	60	5-50
Cape Thompson to Kotzebue	120	
Kotzebue to Noorvik	55	·30
Noorvik to Ruby	260	1·50
Ruby to Fairbanks	250	2-15
TOTAL	1580	17-25

Joe Crosson
PILOT

Robert Lavery
GENERAL MANAGER

area between Wiseman and Barrow through the Brooks Range and the Endicott Mountains. Crosson needed Eielson to show him the way. The Stinsons had more speed and a longer fuel range, so Crosson had to leave before Eielson and Wilkins and refuel at Wiseman. He would then take off from Wiseman to join the Stinsons as they passed overhead on the way to Barrow. It seemed simple.

Crosson and his passenger left Fairbanks on March 25. The March days were getting longer, and sunshine on snow offered a welcome brightness after the dark days of January and February. Along with sunshine came more moderate temperatures. It was 20 degrees below zero in the open cockpit, but this was a big improvement from 40 below or colder. The trip to Wiseman was the brighter part of the journey, because the sun still wouldn't break the horizon in Barrow for weeks.

Landing at Wiseman, Crosson fueled the plane, but had trouble restarting the motor. When it finally started, the radiator boiled over. Crosson found leaks and splits in the radiator that would have to be soldered before he could continue.

Meanwhile, the planes piloted by Eielson and Graham arrived and circled, waiting for Crosson to take off and join them on the flight to Barrow. None of the planes were equipped with radios, and the pilots were puzzled by the delay. They couldn't take a chance on landing with the heavy loads the Stinsons were carrying. Eielson dropped down to take a closer look and Crosson waved them on. Crosson couldn't follow, and Wilkins couldn't wait.

On Wilkins' order, Eielson turned north for Barrow, and Graham

followed. They assumed that Crosson would fly back to Fairbanks after fixing the Super Swallow. But Wilkins had yet to fully appreciate the combination of determination and skill that made up Joe Crosson. Repair would be difficult in the remote location. Wiseman had no hangar to keep the plane and its engine warm. After the Stinsons faded from view, Crosson drained the hot oil and took it into the roadhouse to keep warm until the plane was repaired. He spent the next couple of hours removing the radiator so he could bring it into the roadhouse as well. The citizens of Wiseman offered their tools to the pilot, who worked well into the night soldering the leaks. By morning Joe had placed a tarp over the plane, started a small heater to warm it up, reinstalled the radiator, poured the warm oil back into the motor, and was ready for the day's flight.

Joe and his passenger boarded the Super Swallow and took off. Barrow was 330 miles to the north. Joe relied on the sun's position and his own dead reckoning to pick his course. His magnetic compass was marginal help at best, because the needle pointed between 25 and 30 degrees east of true north—toward the magnetic north pole in Canada, which is hundreds of miles south of the true North Pole. The discrepancy only grew worse minute by minute as Joe traveled farther

▲ *Residents of Wiseman wish Joe and* Detroit News *reporter A. M. Smith good luck as the two men leave for Barrow in the Super Swallow on March 26, 1927. No good maps or navigation aids guided Crosson as he flew high into the Arctic, crossing the Brooks Range.*

▲ The people of Kotzebue greet Joe and the first airplane to ever visit the northern Alaska coastal village. Joe visited Kotzebue on his return flight to Fairbanks after leaving reporter A. M. Smith in Barrow with explorer Hubert Wilkins.

north. He flew on, using what he remembered of Eielson's descriptions and his own best judgment. His sense of direction proved to be uncanny, and after four tense hours, he spotted the tiny Eskimo village of Barrow at the top of Alaska.

In the open cockpit, Joe peered around the frosted windshield to choose a landing site near the village. The temperature had dropped to 40 degrees below zero, and by the time he landed on the ice of the lagoon, his cheeks and lips were frostbitten. Much to the surprise of all, he had crossed the uncharted Brooks Range and managed to find Barrow.

Wilkins was elated. His two planes were fueled and ready to go, the *Detroit News* reporter had arrived, and Wilkins was ready to fly into the high Arctic. Joe Crosson's accomplishment left a lasting impression on the polar explorer.

Wilkins and Eielson completed several flights and at one point were forced down on drifting ice, one hundred miles northeast of Barrow. In the trek back to Barrow, Eielson suffered severe frostbite to his hands. Despite the challenges, their measurements and observations helped scientists learn that there was no land under the polar ice cap.

Two days after he arrived at Barrow, Crosson left to return to Fairbanks. He decided against crossing the Brooks Range a second time and instead chose another uncharted course southwest along the coast of Alaska. He planned to fly to the Yukon River and follow the dogsled trails upstream to Fairbanks. It was 24 degrees below zero.

In flight, the Super Swallow's engine again overheated. This time Crosson was forced to land on the barren ice pack, alone and miles from firewood or shelter. If he shut the plane down he'd have no way to warm the oil and might never get the plane started. But if he didn't get the motor cooled off immediately, it would be ruined and he would be stranded with no chance for rescue. Leaving the engine idling, he grabbed his knife and chipped out pieces of ice small enough to fit into the radiator. He crawled between the skis and slipped the chips into the radiator, mere inches away from the whirling propeller. It worked. The engine cooled down and he was soon ready to go again.

By the time Crosson finally reached Kotzebue, the wind was blowing near gale force. He bounced along the sky and chose a landing spot on sea ice near the village. Excited Eskimos, most of whom had never seen an airplane, swarmed around the plane as he secured it from the wind. He waited for three days for the weather to break. On April 1 the winds finally calmed to the point that he could fly again. He made a short flight to Noorvik and broke a landing gear leg while touching down on the rough river ice. His was the first airplane to ever land at the village. With help from local Eskimos, he worked until after midnight to repair the craft.

The following morning Crosson took off again. He flew inland, refueled at Ruby, and followed the Yukon and Tanana Rivers upstream to the Chena River and into Fairbanks. Weather and visibility again failed to cooperate. He flew the last few miles into Fairbanks just over the railroad tracks, low enough to look moose in the eye.

This incredible winter journey had taken eight days to complete. Crosson had flown over uncharted territory, repaired a radiator and landing gear en route, and introduced Eskimo villages to the airplane. He even delivered a letter in Fairbanks postmarked in Barrow—the first airmail from arctic Alaska.

Leaving the engine idling, he grabbed his knife and chipped out pieces of ice small enough to fit into the radiator. He crawled between the skis and slipped the chips into the radiator, mere inches away from the whirling propeller. It worked. The engine cooled down and he was soon ready to go again.

George King and Joe

6

CHASING THE
MIDNIGHT SUN

Summer 1927. Summer in Interior Alaska is not just a season, it's an event. Wildflowers and cultivated flower gardens explode with color to greet everyone who ventures outside. Days grow brighter and longer until darkness just gives up in June.

As summer arrived, flying returned to a more steady pace at the small field in Fairbanks. Flights to the region's mining operations were starting to become almost commonplace. The flights saved miners weeks of difficult overland travel to and from their claims. They were more than willing to pay.

Many of the landings Crosson and the other pilots made nearly every day in Alaska would be considered extremely risky by today's standards. They often landed on river gravel bars or on ridge tops. The risks were compounded by miners who didn't fully understand aviation and assumed that planes could land in any relatively cleared area. One such overly optimistic miner went by the name of Van Curler.

Van Curler arrived at Rickert's Field in June 1927, looking for a pilot to fly him to his mine on Palmer Creek, seventy-five miles from Fairbanks. He found Joe Crosson. The miner assured the pilot that he

May 20-21, 1927

Charles A. Lindbergh makes the first solo, nonstop trans-Atlantic flight.

◄ *Joe Crosson and his friend George King (left) check out one of the odd-looking tractors brought to Alaska for the 1926 Detroit Arctic Expedition by Hubert Wilkins, to haul supplies across the snow.*

had a good landing field at his place and Crosson agreed to fly. Then he actually saw the strip. In his words, it was "nothing but a potato patch, maybe 350 foot long, right in the middle of the river." Van Curler insisted that Joe's friend Ben Eielson had easily and safely landed there. Joe decided to chance a landing in the old Jenny.

After a last good look, Joe set up a landing and glided down toward the potato patch. "I came in a little short," he remembered. "Wham!

The ship turned over on its back." The motor noise ended abruptly, and amid only the sounds of the river, creaks and groans from the plane, and the gurgles of fuel dribbling onto the ground, Van Curler and his supplies spilled and tumbled out of the plane. The miner's wife had been watching, and she hurried across the river in a boat. No one was hurt, but the plane was upside down with a bent propeller.

Pleased that everyone escaped injury, the couple seemed unconcerned about the accident. "Don't you worry, we'll have her fixed in a jiffy," Van Curler told Joe. With that the industrious couple went to work. From two poles and a cable they built a windlass and attached the cable to the plane. All three strained at the crank and slowly but surely got the old Jenny back on its landing gear. Van Curler and his wife weren't particularly concerned about the bent propeller, either. Joe recalled that the woman held a log behind the prop while the two men pounded it out to where it cleared the engine.

Joe knew the old bird was in rough shape, but he hoped she was still somewhat airworthy. He was ready to try to fly back to Fairbanks, but the plane had lost so much fuel he didn't think he could make it. Once more the ingenious couple came to the rescue. They filled the Jenny's tank with ten gallons of lamp gas. Joe remembered the rest of the trip:

"I got in and tried the engine. She was rough, but I let her wind up and took off. Oh boy, that old engine was really jumping around, but I wheeled in to Fairbanks careful as I could, landed, put the ship in a hangar, shut the doors, and never told anyone."

The trip to Van Curler's so-called airstrip, like that to Joe Quigley's the previous summer, drove home a valuable lesson. From that day on Crosson relied exclusively on his own judgment to choose areas safe for landing.

~

BACK IN FAIRBANKS, Crosson spent time repairing the Jenny. He next flew the old craft on the Fourth of July with his friend and flight student George King.

"I got in and tried the engine. She was rough, but I let her wind up and took off. Oh boy, that old engine was really jumping around, but I wheeled in to Fairbanks careful as I could, landed, put the ship in a hangar, shut the doors, and never told anyone."

◄ *Nellie Ross Norwood prepares to travel with Joe to the Episcopal Mission at Fort Yukon. The flying trip took mere hours, compared with the alternative of days of travel on the Chena, Tanana, and Yukon Rivers.*

Joe's logbook includes several notes of "Instructions to George King," and in June, George soloed after only a few hours of flight training.

George was one of the first people Joe Crosson met in Fairbanks. When Joe first set foot in Interior Alaska, George was already a regular at Rickert's Field, watching the activity surrounding Hubert Wilkins' first assault on the North Pole in 1926. For a while Joe and George shared a cabin as roommates.

George shared a love of flying and a spark of adventure with the aviators. He and Joe took pictures of each other on the peculiar-looking tractors that Wilkins had planned to use for hauling fuel to Barrow for the polar flight. (Because the tractors couldn't haul much weight and consumed a great deal of fuel, they proved to be more of a conversation piece than a useful tool for the expedition.)

George was a hard-working and adventurous prospector by trade, but he longed to fly. He worked for the Territory of Alaska during the summer of 1926, building runways, and in 1927 as a mechanic for the Fairbanks Airplane Corporation. Joe's logbook includes several notes of "Instructions to George King," and in June, George soloed after only a few hours of flight training.

July Fourth was a highlight of summer. Endless sunny days and warm evenings energized miners and townsfolk alike. Miners and their families traveled on the narrow-gauge railroad from mining camps to Fairbanks for the festivities, and an air of anticipation blanketed the town. Always the adventurer, Joe came up with a plan to increase the excitement: he decided to put on an air show with a spectacular finale, and George King was game to assist his mentor.

▶ The young, clean-cut kid from San Diego and the experienced prospector and adventurer George King became fast-friends. King taught Joe Crosson about Alaska and Joe taught King to fly.

Earlier in the summer Joe had found an old parachute in the company hangar. The parachute hadn't been used in years, and Joe didn't know if it would work. Neither of the men was willing to be the guinea pig, so they attached the chute's harness to a sandbag. Joe put it in the Jenny and flew to the right altitude, where he dropped the dummy while George watched from the ground. The parachute seemed to work fine, and that was enough for Joe. About three weeks later he wore the parachute as he went up in the Jenny with fellow pilot Ed Young. At 3,500 feet, Fairbanks looked rather small as Joe climbed out on the lower wing of the plane. The last time he had done this, he was over San Diego and his sister Marvel was at the controls. He stood for a moment in the prop wash, looking over Rickert's Field, then jumped and floated to the ground. He landed safely in the brush next to the field.

When the Fourth of July arrived, it was sunny and warm. With George King as passenger, Joe thrilled the cheering crowd by guiding the Jenny through loops, barrel rolls, Immelman turns, side slips, spins, and other maneuvers. The high point of the hour-long show came when George climbed out on the wing, let go, and floated beneath the parachute to the ground.

No one is sure why Joe jumped earlier in the summer, or how George came to give it a try at the air show. It might have been sheer curiosity. Perhaps Joe viewed it as another kind of flying. Whatever the reason, any fascination with parachutes must have been satisfied. Joe never jumped again.

~

CROSSON CONTINUED to fly in the Interior during July 1927. His fame both within the Territory

Perhaps Joe viewed it as another kind of flying. Whatever the reason, any fascination with parachutes must have been satisfied. Joe never jumped again.

as well as in the forty-eight states was growing. Inspired by the young pilot's reputation, a doctor from Alabama announced to his friends, "I'm going to Fairbanks, Alaska, and have Joe Crosson take me up for a look at the midnight sun."

Crosson loaded his eager passenger into the Super Swallow biplane at dusk during a clear summer evening. He took off and skillfully climbed the craft high enough to see the sun, which had dipped below the horizon. At 14,600 feet the incredible view of the sun at midnight and the brisk high-altitude air gave the doctor even more of a thrill than he had anticipated. Back on the ground, he stated, "Climbing up into the sky to arouse old Sol from his bed was about the most wonderful thing I've done in my life."

A week later, Crosson set an Alaska altitude record in the Super Swallow by climbing to 17,500 feet with a tourist from Hawaii for another peek at the midnight sun.

Later that summer at Wiseman, local miners had a surprise in store for Crosson. They voted him an honorary member of the Pioneers of Alaska. Full membership in the Pioneers is restricted to the hardy and self-sufficient few who have proven themselves over thirty years' time in the Territory. The respect and trust the miners placed in Crosson was evident, because at that time he had lived in Alaska for less than a year and a half.

In August, Crosson and George King left Alaska on a working vacation to visit the Crosson family in San Diego and check out new airplanes that might be useful in the Territory. Crosson test-flew planes in San Diego, Los Angeles, and Spokane, Washington. He also met airplane designer and builder Eddie Stinson, and dined with Martin Jennings and Art Goebel, winners of the Dole prize for making the first flight from San Francisco to Honolulu. Crosson and King were part of the crowd that watched Jimmy Doolittle at the Spokane air races.

Following the excitement, Crosson returned to Alaska while King remained in the continental United States. Crosson's traveling companion on the trip back north was the pilot he knew and trusted better than anyone else: his sister Marvel.

◄ Joe prepares to take a
parachute jump in June
1927. Joe had found the
old chute, which had
been used in an
exhibition during 1924,
in the back of a hangar.
He tested it with weights
before trying it himself.

Lillian Osborne and Marvel

7

MARVEL AND LILLIAN

Autumn 1927. Two women were Joe Crosson's partners and confidantes. One was his lovely sister, Marvel. The other was Lillian Osborne, a fiercely independent young beauty who became his wife.

Lillian was born in Seattle in 1908. Her parents lived in Cordova, Alaska, a rough-and-tumble railroad and fishing town that offered little in the way of medical care, so her mother traveled south for Lillian's birth. Her Norwegian-born father was a renowned jeweler who followed gold rushes across Alaska, eventually settling in Cordova. Lillian's mother was a quiet Norwegian woman who met her husband-to-be on board ship when she emigrated from Oslo, Norway.

Life in small pioneer towns encouraged self sufficiency, and Lillian learned to take care of herself. While she was still quite young, her parents separated and she moved with her mother to Anchorage, then Seward, and finally Seattle. When Lillian was just fourteen years old, her mother died. By the time she was fifteen she was working on her own and responsible for herself.

When Lillian turned eighteen, she moved back to Cordova and contemplated her future. Her father had remarried and was planning to move his family to Juneau. Lillian decided against going to Juneau and moved in with the family of her friend Doris McConnell. She went

October 19, 1927

Pan American Airways opens its first scheduled service with flights between Key West, Florida, and Havana, Cuba, a distance of ninety miles.

◄ *College student Lillian Osborne (left) and pilot Marvel Crosson in their fur parkas were the darlings of aviators when they visited the airport at Weeks Field in Fairbanks.*

*At some point, Wheatley
decided that Lillian
Osborne should meet
the handsome young
pilot Joe Crosson.*

to work as an operator with "Mac" McConnell's telephone company, working the midnight to 6:00 a.m. shift. She also did office work for a lawyer and spent some time working in a crab cannery. Doris McConnell decided to attend the Alaska Agricultural College and School of Mines in Fairbanks. Although money was tight, Lillian decided she would attend too. She was used to working and confident she could find employment to pay for room, board, and school. Lillian enrolled and planned to move to Fairbanks in September 1927.

Lillian had natural talent for dancing. She lacked formal training, but loved to move to music. Small towns of the day hosted shows of local talent for entertainment, and Lillian impressed many people with her grace and movement as she danced in the shows. During one of the rehearsals, piano player Don Adler waited for Lillian to give him instructions and to explain her dance routine, as the other performers were doing. Adler was impressed when she merely asked him to play whatever he wanted, then spontaneously and beautifully danced to his music. Another person who took note of Lillian was dance instructor Cuba Wheatley.

Wheatley made a living traveling around the western states and Alaska teaching dance, and she made many trips through the major towns of Alaska during the late 1920s. July of 1927 found her in Cordova teaching the latest dances, including the Charleston and the black bottom, to a group of eager young pupils that included Lillian and Doris. When she learned that the girls were headed north to Fairbanks for college, Wheatley shared tales of the town and the people she had met there. The teacher came to appreciate the initiative, character, and potential shown by Lillian. At some point, Wheatley decided that Lillian Osborne should meet the handsome young pilot Joe Crosson.

A week or so later Wheatley was in Fairbanks. At the time, Joe Crosson and George King were getting ready to head out of the Territory on their working vacation to California. A trip "outside" in those days was not a minor undertaking. The most common route out of Interior Alaska included a two-day train trip from Fairbanks to Seward, then passage on a steamship with stops at Cordova and

Southeast Alaska towns on the way to Seattle. It isn't clear who Wheatley spoke with to plant the idea of looking up Lillian in Cordova, but when their ship arrived, that's exactly what Joe and George tried to do. However, when they called, Lillian was asleep, getting rested for her night job. Later in the day, Doris told Lillian about the handsome young pilot who had been looking for her.

At smaller seaports it was customary for residents to gather at the dock to greet ships coming and going. As a crowd from town gathered to wish this steamship bon voyage, Lillian was there. A friend pointed out the dashing Crosson. With boldness brought on by youth and her approaching move to the college town, Lillian flirted with the handsome aviator. "Yoo hoo, I'll see you in Fairbanks!" she cried as she waved. Joe smiled, but was embarrassed by attention from females to whom he'd not yet been introduced.

▲ *Marvel Crosson logged flying time in the Alaskan skies during late 1927 and early 1928. In 1928 Marvel earned her limited commercial pilot license after taking a check-ride with aviator Ben Eielson.*

▲ *Pilot Noel Wien (left),
Lillian Osborne, Marvel
Crosson, and Pathé News
photographer Earl
Rossman get together at
Weeks Field in Fairbanks.
Wien gave Lillian—Joe
Crosson's bride to be—
her first ride in an
airplane, while Joe was
out of the Territory.*

~

AS THE DOCKS of Cordova faded from view, Joe had much to think about. There was that attractive young woman in Cordova, the mystery that his future held, and back in San Diego the person who shared his dreams, his older sister Marvel.

When the offer for employment in Alaska had come to Joe during 1926, Marvel stayed behind in San Diego. She held a job as head of the dinnerware department at a major department store, but most of her free time was devoted to flying. She was one of the first women to choose commercial aviation as a career. With Joe she dreamed of creating a family business that would include maintaining and repairing planes, teaching flying, and making commercial trips. They would be joined by their younger sister Zelma, who intended to learn to fly after completing high school.

Marvel was a bit of a pet among the flyers at Dutch Flats, the San

Diego airfield where she continued to fly. Instead of considering her just a pretty young woman, she was respected as one of the best pilots. The San Diego newspaper described Marvel as "so steeped in aviation that she carries you into the clouds the moment you speak with her."

Joe had left her behind, but not for long. They were kindred spirits. It would have been unnatural if Marvel had not gone north to join her younger brother. So when Joe headed back to Alaska, Marvel was with him.

Marvel sold the little Jenny that she and Joe had bought and rebuilt years earlier and headed for Alaska with Joe in October 1927. Two weeks of travel on steamships and trains allowed her to catch up with her brother's adventures and bring him up to date about her own in greater detail than in their exchanges of letters. Temperatures on the trip were much colder than during any winter she had experienced in San Diego, but adventure was worth the price.

Marvel soon settled into the gold-mining town of Fairbanks. Her experience taking aerial photographs with Joe in San Diego led to a job with Cann's Photography Studio. She learned about cold weather and how to dress to stay warm, and by the time real winter set in, she was a regular fixture at Rickert's Field.

Marvel surveyed her new surroundings and the community while Joe returned to the growing aviation business in Alaska. With the seasonal change from chilly, foggy, late-fall mornings to the snowy-white days of early winter, Joe again made the transition from landing on wheels to landing on skis.

The San Diego newspaper described Marvel as "so steeped in aviation that she carries you into the clouds the moment you speak with her."

～

THAT SAME AUTUMN, Lillian Osborne moved north to attend college with Doris McConnell. Students from the southern parts of Alaska rode a steamship to Seward, then the Alaska Railroad to Fairbanks. The train buzzed with activity as students from Ketchikan, Juneau, Cordova, Seward, and Anchorage got to know each other. About forty young men lived in the men's dormitory on the campus of the Alaska Agricultural College and School of Mines. Lillian and Doris were two

▶ *Marvel (left) and Lillian share a moment of fun at the cabin Marvel rented in Fairbanks.*

of only seven females who lived in the dorm for women. According to Lillian, President Charles Bunnell "watched over us like a hawk" and strictly enforced a curfew. He regularly interrupted breakfast by

announcing to the entire student body which of the students had been
caught staying out late the night before.

Mining was the main course of study, but students could take a
variety of different classes. Lillian chose business courses, which
allowed her to work as a secretary and in accounting. Doris, who was
extremely athletic, planned to play on the women's basketball team,
which was scheduled to travel around the Territory to play games.
Doris desperately wanted Lillian to go on the trips, so she talked her
friend into trying out for the team. At five feet, two inches, Lillian
certainly wasn't the best candidate to be a player. Doris put her
through many nights of practice, sometimes until midnight, shooting
basket after basket until Lillian thought her arms would drop off, but
in the end she made the team as a substitute.

Fairbanks in 1927 was a small but thriving gold mining town of a
few thousand people. Entertainment was an important part of
community life, and residents flocked to the movie theater, parties,
concerts, and dances. Lillian was young, vibrant, single, and beautiful.
She was not a wallflower, and her dance card was quick to fill. Weekly
dances found her gliding across the floor with pilots, miners, and other
eligible young bachelors.

At one winter dance at Eagle's Hall, her card featured the name of
the handsome Joe Crosson. Lillian was attending with her friend Jack
Boswell, but she noticed the flyer right away and was disappointed to
see that he was already escorting a pretty lady. She was relieved to learn
that the lady was his sister Marvel. Lillian must have made an
impression, because before the evening was over Joe had promised to
take her flying for the first time.

Before he could make good on his promise, Joe planned another
trip to the continental United States. He'd barely had time to introduce
Marvel to the pilots and mechanics at the airfield before he departed
Fairbanks in December 1927. This time he planned to raise money for
an airline venture he envisioned for Alaska.

Joe asked Marvel to contact Lillian at the college and explain that
the plane ride he promised would have to be postponed. Marvel did as
Joe asked, and immediately took a liking to the young student. Lillian

Lillian was young, vibrant, single, and beautiful. She was not a wallflower, and her dance card was quick to fill. Weekly dances found her gliding across the floor with pilots, miners, and other eligible young bachelors.

Ben Eielson, a Department of Commerce check pilot, gave Marvel a check-ride and signed her off for a limited commercial pilot's license, making her not only the first woman licensed to fly in Alaska, but also the first female pilot who could legally carry passengers in the Territory.

found aviation enthralling, and she was fascinated with Marvel and her experiences flying. Marvel adopted Lillian as a little sister and invited the student to stay with her in Fairbanks on weekends. Before long they were close friends who enjoyed much of the entertainment that Fairbanks had to offer.

~

YOUNG PEOPLE who shared a love of airplanes and flight were a tight-knit crew. Marvel's cabin became a social gathering place for pilots and aviation aficionados, who spent hours "hangar flying." Beautiful young women did not go unnoticed in Fairbanks in the 1920s, and especially not in the aviation world. Marvel and Lillian were the object of much attention. Lillian received her first plane ride from Noel Wien before Joe returned, and she became good friends with Ben Eielson and the other pilots. Marvel caught Ben Eielson's eye, and that of virtually every other single pilot in the Territory, including Noel Wien. But she wasn't looking for a husband and wasn't interested in settling down. She just wanted to keep flying.

Without an airplane of her own, Marvel had a formidable task. Airplanes were scarce in Alaska. But Marvel's tenacity (and no doubt her single status) helped. She flew with the other pilots in the region and built time in her logbook. She flew short hops locally, and she flew hundreds of miles away to Anchorage and Nome. Marvel's flights during 1927 and 1928 were the first by a female pilot in the Territory of Alaska. Ben Eielson, a Department of Commerce check pilot, gave her a check-ride and signed her off for a limited commercial pilot's license, making her not only the first woman licensed to fly in Alaska, but also the first female pilot who could legally carry passengers in the Territory.

Like Joe, Marvel was becoming widely known; her star was rising. The early spring of 1928 was fun-filled and exciting. In March, Marvel shivered at the controls of the open-cockpit Waco owned by Noel Wien. The temperature was 40 degrees below zero even before the engine started blasting the frigid air over her fur flying suit. She flew to three mining camps and helped deliver cargo before returning to

◄ Marvel Crosson stands on an ice floe in the Chena River during spring breakup in 1928. When the winter freeze on the rivers of Interior Alaska begins to thaw, the banks are choked with ice grinding its way downstream for days.

Rickert's Field. In spite of the cold she had to smile. This was a far cry from the sunny, warm, relatively carefree flying she had experienced in San Diego. But Alaska allowed Marvel to broaden her piloting skills by learning how to keep airplanes functional in extreme cold and how to maneuver a plane on skis.

The story of Marvel's flying in Alaska was too much for the national media to pass up. Or, for that matter, to get right. Newspapers across the United States carried stories of the "Flying Grocery Girl" and her exploits carrying supplies across the Alaska wilderness to remote mining camps. Reporters were enthralled with the beautiful pilot—so much so that reports of routine flights were enhanced and glamorized to include stories of rescue flights and other airborne heroics. The truth was tamer.

She logged less than fifty hours in the Territory, but she was truly a pioneer. The flying that Marvel did in Alaska gained her national recognition. By the time she left Fairbanks, Marvel's legend was larger than life. Her fame opened doors of opportunity that probably would have stayed closed had she remained in California.

Joe in Antarctica

8

ANTARCTIC PILOT

Spring 1928. The demand for aviation was increasing in the Territory. Even though relatively few people lived in Interior Alaska, it was apparent to the pilots that a regional airline could efficiently serve the region. Joe Crosson, Ben Eielson, and George King shared the airline vision. Knowing investors would be needed, the men formed a company with that goal in mind. Crosson believed money could be raised more readily outside of Alaska where more people routinely depended on flying and where airlines were growing rapidly.

With Marvel settled into Fairbanks for the winter, Crosson traveled to Seattle and then to the East Coast seeking investors for a larger and more efficient flying company. A young Alaskan pilot was a novel sight in the board rooms of the East Coast, but Joe's attempts to attract capital were not immediately successful. Dreams of an Alaska airline didn't materialize, and over the winter Crosson ran low on money. By March 1928, with funds exhausted, he was back in the air flying for wages.

Years later, he recalled: "After spending some time in New York on this venture and needing funds, I took a job with the Fokker Airplane Company from Teterboro to Winnipeg. Shortly thereafter I went to work for the Western Canada Airways, first ferrying ships from the factory to the field of operation and later flying within Canada. . . ."

May 31-June 10, 1928
Captain Kingsford Smith makes the first flight between the United States and Australia, in a Fokker F-7 flying from California to Hawaii and Fiji before arriving in Brisbane.

◄ *A resident of the Antarctic greets Joe Crosson. Curious penguins were on hand when the flyers arrived in 1928.*

79

After waiting out several days of bad weather in Barrow, Wilkins and Eielson took off from a frozen lagoon and successfully flew across the polar sea to Spitsbergen, Norway, on the other side of the planet.

Flying in Canada increased Joe's proficiency level and added to his knowledge of northern flying. Western Canada Airways used huge Fokker Universals to supply gold mining operations. Taking advantage of the extensive system of lakes in Ontario, the company operated the aircraft on floats. Working at a hurried pace during the long summer sunshine, Joe's flying days often included a dozen or more water landings in a single day. His reputation and skill as a bush pilot served him well.

While Joe busied himself outside of Alaska, Hubert Wilkins and Ben Eielson had returned to Fairbanks during February 1928 to prepare for another arctic flight. This time they were in a new Lockheed Vega. Leaving Rickert's Field on March 20, they again gained the attention of the world. After waiting out several days of bad weather in Barrow, the pair took off from a frozen lagoon and successfully flew across the polar sea to Spitsbergen, Norway, on the other side of the planet.

The success of this flight made news throughout the world. Wilkens and Eielson were now aviation and polar giants. They were guests of the king of Norway at a reception in their honor, and Wilkins was knighted by the king of England. The explorer then set his sights on the other end of the earth.

~

ANTARCTICA WAS THE least-known continent on the planet. Hubert Wilkins knew that better maps were needed of Antarctica, and he planned to conduct aerial photography to increase the world's knowledge of the continent. Success of the Lockheed Vega in the Arctic made it an obvious choice for the Antarctic. But the selection of pilots to handle aircraft near the South Pole was a critical decision.

During his three expeditions to the Arctic, Wilkins had gauged the ability of his men carefully. The remote Antarctic required that he choose only the most skilled and capable men. His small crew was put together from the rosters of previous expeditions. For the critical positions of lead mechanic and pilots he chose three Alaskans: Orville Porter, Ben Eielson, and Joe Crosson.

Porter was a skilled aircraft mechanic who went to Fairbanks with

◄ *Aviation gas for the Antarctic flights was carried in rectangular, metal five-gallon cans. Wooden crates held two cans each.*

▲ *The two Lockheed Vega airplanes used on Hubert Wilkins' 1928 Antarctic expedition perch secured aboard the freighter Southern Cross during the long trip south.*

the Stinson Detroiters during the 1927 expedition and stayed on in the north. Eielson had been with Wilkins from the beginning, flying during all three northern expeditions. He also needed Joe Crosson. Wilkins had marked him as a trustworthy pilot in 1927 when Crosson ferried a *Detroit News* reporter from Fairbanks to Barrow in an open-cockpit plane over uncharted territory, complete with mechanical repairs en route.

Wilkins needed the talents of all three Alaskans to ensure this undertaking. The three were friends, and Wilkins engaged in a bit of deception to make sure all three would accept the challenge. His method was simple. He simultaneously sent Porter, Eielson, and Crosson telegrams telling each that the other two had agreed to go on the expedition. They all accepted.

One Lockheed Vega was not sufficient. The expedition would use two of the craft fitted with wheels, skis, or pontoons as needed so flights could be based out of the ice pack, snowfields, or open sea. Wilkins still had the Vega that was used on the northern polar flight. The second was to be flown directly from the factory in California to New York, where the expedition would depart. Crosson was entrusted with picking up the new plane, testing it, and delivering it to New York.

Crosson was working as a pilot in Canada on August 22, 1928, when he got the telegram from Wilkins. He immediately wired Marvel in Fairbanks, asking her to meet him in Los Angeles right away. He gave no reason for the request, and Marvel wondered what was up. She had just begun to feel at home in Fairbanks, and Joe was asking her to leave on short notice. But she immediately agreed to go. Marvel settled her affairs in Fairbanks, headed south, and arrived in Los Angeles on September 11.

Joe picked up the Vega at the Lockheed factory. Brother and sister pilots were reunited. They flew to San Diego together the following day. Their parents, Esler and Elizabeth Crosson, met them at the airport and the family spent a busy hour together while the Vega was serviced. The reunion was brief but joyful in the warm Southern California sun. Elizabeth had prepared a large basket of food for Joe and Marvel to enjoy during the long flight to New York, including roast chicken, sandwiches, and fruit. After a loving goodbye, the younger Crossons were off to the East Coast.

They flew to El Paso the first day, St. Louis the second, and reached Long Island the third evening. Joe and Marvel checked into the Waldorf Astoria and surprised Wilkins more than a full day ahead of schedule on September 15. Favorable winds and high performance weren't the reasons for the swift trip; it was thanks to the fact that Marvel had shared the flying duties. When Joe tired he turned the ship over to Marvel and slept, trusting her fully with the valuable craft and the fate of the Antarctic expedition. The new Lockheed was loaded onto the freighter *Southern Cross*. After seeing the explorer and his crew off, Marvel headed back to California.

The Antarctic expedition called for a stop in Montevideo, Uruguay, then on to the Falkland Islands, and finally to Antarctica. A long ocean voyage was something new for the aviators. As their camaraderie

When Joe tired he turned the ship over to Marvel and slept, trusting her fully with the valuable craft and the fate of the Antarctic expedition.

▲ Joe Crosson and Ben Eielson look more like businessmen than bush pilots in this publicity photo for the Wilkins expedition to the Antarctic.

deepened, they all stopped shaving and grew beards. They watched as mariners marked their first crossing of the equator by shaving their heads. The presence of women on the ship apparently discouraged the Alaskans from joining in that tradition. However, after arriving in Antarctica, Crosson and Porter decided to shave their heads, in part to make Eielson (who was already balding) feel better, and Eielson joined in as well. The three men made a curious sight: a trio of baldheaded, bushy-bearded Alaskans in Antarctica. (Joe's mother was not impressed with his Antarctic appearance. A year later, Elizabeth Crosson saw photos of the hairless expedition crew in a store window in San Diego. She marched into the store and demanded that the manager remove the photos, and he did.)

The trip to Montevideo and the Falklands was uneventful, but when still three hundred miles from their final destination, Wilkins found pack ice was blocking his passage to the intended anchorage at Deception Island. The *Southern Cross* could not make it through the ice, but a whaling vessel, the *Hektoria*, broke a path for Wilkins' ship.

Weather and rough pack ice made unloading the planes at Deception Island a difficult task. The first days of flying on the Antarctic continent were far from routine. Initial flights were made from the sea ice, but warming summer temperatures undermined the safety of the makeshift runway. Early in the expedition Eielson landed his plane on skis near the supply ship. Wilkins had marked out an area where the ice was thick enough to support the weight of the airplane. The makeshift runway was so slippery that when Eielson landed, the Vega slid past the safe zone and onto rotting ice. The crew watched, horrified, as the ice gave way and swallowed the landing gear and the motor of the plane.

They held their breath as Eielson cautiously climbed out and made his way to safe ice. He was unhurt, but the plane was in a perilous position. The craft was hanging by one wing and part of the fuselage. Under the flimsy ice was twelve hundred feet of frigid water. Joe was airborne in the other Vega and had watched the drama unfold. Unable to help his friend, he circled the site and flew back to the crude runway on Deception Island to get help.

▲ *Joe sports the bald look adopted by himself, fellow pilot Ben Eielson, and mechanic Orville Porter when they arrived in Antarctica.*

Joe rallied the whalers to once again help the expedition. Quick thinking and ingenuity were needed to save the Vega from a watery grave. Ropes were carefully attached to the tail, and the plane was jacked up using levers and wooden planks for blocking. More than once the ice gave way and would-be rescuers were pulled from the cold water. Finally, long planks were slid under the skis and the Vega was dragged back to safe ice. Eighteen hours of backbreaking work had allowed Wilkins' crew to continue their quest.

Mechanics cleaned salt water from the engine, and they attached floats to the plane so that it could operate in water. When the time came to get the plane back into the air, Crosson was called upon. He fired up the engine, opened the throttle, and inched the Vega along the

Joe rallied the whalers to once again help the expedition. Eighteen hours of backbreaking work allowed Wilkins' crew to continue their quest.

pack ice. The scraping noise of ice on metal reverberated through the pontoons as the plane picked up speed. Everyone breathed easier when the unnatural scraping abruptly gave way to motor noise as the plane became airborne. The sense of relief was short-lived. As Joe maneuvered to land in open water next to the ship, the Vega hit a flock of birds. There was no permanent damage to plane or pilot, but in a short span of time both Eielson and Crosson had narrowly avoided disaster.

The remaining flights in the Antarctic were, by comparison, uneventful. Wilkins and Eielson made several photographic flights and recorded minor discoveries. Overall, the expedition was a success. Wilkins had proven airplanes could operate at the bottom of the earth.

The Alaskans again boarded a ship for the long voyage back to the United States. As they cleaned up their appearance, getting ready for civilization, Crosson's sense of humor took over. He appeared at dinner one evening with his own beard trimmed and clipped to an exact replica of Sir Hubert Wilkins' own goatee. The explorer looked sharply

at Joe, but didn't utter a word. Joe was embarrassed, excused himself, and returned to the dinner a short time later, clean shaven.

Wilkins would return to the Antarctic to fly again the following year, but with a new crew. The Alaskan pilots had other plans. Eielson stayed in New York until he found financial backers to start a regional airline in Alaska. The new company, Alaskan Airways, was formed by purchasing small aviation companies already established in the Territory. Eielson was back in Alaska before the end of summer in 1929.

Crosson spent a good bit of his time in 1929 ferrying planes for Lockheed, in Oklahoma, California, Texas, Kansas, Michigan, Ohio, Wisconsin, Utah, New York, Illinois, Arizona, and New Mexico. During one flight from Oklahoma to California he picked up a hitchhiking pilot who became a close friend and a famous figure, Wiley Post.

Sandwiched between his paying flights were trips to San Diego to meet Marvel. She had made quite a name during his absence and now had even bigger plans.

◄ *A ski-equipped Lockheed Vega sits on the Antarctic continent. Changing seasons and weather conditions required the mixed use of skis, wheels, and pontoons on the expedition's planes.*

Marvel in the Ryan

9

STAR OF THE CLOUDS

San Diego, California, early 1929. As a beautiful young woman pilot who had caught the attention of the national press, Marvel Crosson gave reporters plenty of good copy. She had flown in Alaska, she was intelligent, fun, and ambitious, and she spoke of flying as if it were magic.

Marvel told one reporter: "There is nothing in the world to rest your body after a long, tiresome day at work like a flight in an airplane above the clouds. A sail into the great blue expanse of the heavens, playing hide and seek with the clouds, inspires and rests you, and you return to work, invigorated and rejuvenated."

The days of struggling to scrape together gas money to keep an old plane flying were gone. Since her return to San Diego from Alaska, and her flight to New York in the Vega with Joe, opportunities to fly newer, modern aircraft presented themselves to Marvel. She now found sponsors eager to fund her growing flying goals. In the age of record-setting flights, Marvel set her sights high, very high. She wanted to set the women's altitude record, then held by Louise Thaden, who had climbed to 20,270 feet.

The Union Oil Company of California sponsored Marvel in her attempts to break the record, and provided her a state-of-the-art aircraft to fly—an open-cockpit, 300-horsepower Travel Air.

February 12, 1928
Charles "Speed" Holman flies 1,093 continuous loops at Minneapolis to set a new record for the maneuver.

◄ *Marvel Crosson smiles from the cockpit of the Ryan Brougham she used to set the women's altitude record. She is holding part of the improvised high-altitude oxygen system that was provided to her by members of the Los Angeles Fire Department.*

The official attempts to break altitude records were supervised
by the National Aeronautical Association. Pilots carried a carefully
calibrated and sealed barograph (altimeter) in the plane. Although
pilots could get a general idea of the altitude through a small window
on the container, the exact altitude reached wasn't known until the
barograph was sent to the Bureau of Standards at Washington, D.C.,

where it was opened and the record verified. Marvel's first attempts were made in February 1929 from Clover Field at Santa Monica, California.

Marvel first got into the Travel Air on February 4, and not one to waste time, took it to 19,000 feet the second time she flew the craft. On that flight she expected thinner air at higher altitudes and wasn't sure how it would affect her. She also expected colder temperatures as she climbed, so she layered coveralls and a thin leather jacket over her silk dress.

Although she was prepared for cold temperatures, she didn't expect the bone-chilling minus-20-degree cold of an Alaska winter—but she found it at 19,000 feet. The last time she'd experienced such extreme temperatures, she was wearing a fur flying suit. This time her hands and feet were numb from cold. The pilot's seat was directly in the prop wash of the giant motor. Marvel couldn't feel her face, and she shivered violently. She managed to get the plane back down and landed safely, but when she shut down the Travel Air, she needed help to climb out of the plane. As feeling returned to her hands and feet, her spirits improved. She was very pleased with the flight. The Travel Air had performed perfectly and the Wright Whirlwind motor had plenty of climb left in it.

Three days later Marvel showed up at Clover Field for another attempt on the record. This time she was dressed in a fur-lined flight suit complete with her heavy fur boots from Alaska. For the first time in her flying career she wore a parachute. At two o'clock in the afternoon Marvel fired up the big plane and taxied out to the runway. As the powerful bird ambled along, she studied a new addition to the plane, a simple oxygen system. The mask and tank were on loan from the Los Angeles Fire Department and had been installed in the cockpit by firefighters. Marvel took off and started climbing. Despite the fact that she was better prepared to break the record, it wasn't to be that day. She could only coax the craft to 19,800 feet on the official recording barograph, about 500 feet short of the record. After landing Marvel wasted little time in disappointment. She thought over the quest and promised cheerfully, "Well, we'll do it next time."

This time her hands and feet were numb from cold. The pilot's seat was directly in the prop wash of the giant motor. Marvel couldn't feel her face, and she shivered violently. She managed to get the plane back down and landed safely, but when she shut down the Travel Air, she needed help to climb out of the plane.

◄ *Marvel drinks a cup of coffee while being interviewed by reporters after establishing the women's altitude record at 23,996 feet on May 28, 1929. She beat the previous record by more than 3,700 feet.*

Marvel landed first in Oakland, the winner. Her name and face were becoming a regular feature in newspapers across America. With a racing victory under her belt, Marvel turned again to the altitude record.

Before making another attempt at the altitude record, Marvel continued to fly a variety of aircraft. Her logbook recorded flights in Boeing, Eaglerock, Ryan, Waco, and Ford airplanes. She also had the opportunity to fly with other well-known pilots. In the California skies, she shared flight controls with British aviatrix Lady Heath. She also flew with Emory Bronte, who was famous for navigating the first civilian flight between California and Hawaii. She and Emory shared common interests and became very close.

Her famous brother Joe was back in the continental United States, enjoying the flying in climates warmer than the Antarctic. Their paths crossed several times and they flew together. With Joe's encouragement and assistance, Marvel entered her first air race.

The first National Aeronautics Association Women's Air Race was scheduled for April 20 in California. The course over San Francisco Bay between Palo Alto and Oakland was short, but in 1929 it was one of the few flying contests open to women pilots. Marvel landed first in Oakland, the winner. Her name and face were becoming a regular feature in newspapers across America. With a racing victory under her belt, Marvel turned again to the altitude record.

Union Oil Company this time provided her with a new 300-horsepower Ryan Brougham cabin monoplane, complete with cabin heat. Again Marvel had an oxygen supply installed by members of the Los Angeles Fire Department. Two oxygen tanks with control valves were connected with a rubber hose outfitted with a pipe stem, which Marvel held between her teeth in order to receive oxygen during the flight. The plane carried two recording barographs. One was the sealed instrument calibrated by the Bureau of Standards and opened in Washington, D.C., following the flight to verify the altitude. The other was an older model that Marvel planned to watch while she flew.

Marvel first tried out the new Ryan in early May 1929 and flew it nine times to gain proficiency in the craft. Weather was critical: winds needed to be calm for the record attempt. The Ryan sat ready for the flight at Mines Field in Los Angeles for several days, waiting for the elements to cooperate. Flying weather was poor early in the morning of May 28, so Marvel arrived at the field dressed only in street clothes.

But the winds calmed, and when she learned that conditions looked good, she pulled on coveralls and climbed into the plane. The bright Union Oil logo on the side of the plane made it stand out from all others as she pointed the craft skyward just after eleven in the morning. Within minutes Marvel and the Ryan disappeared upward into the haze.

▲ *Marvel poses with the Travel Air Speedwing Chaparral she flew during the first Women's Air Derby.*

Slowly and methodically the Ryan climbed. At 20,000 feet Marvel was confident the record was hers. At 22,000 feet the outside temperature registered minus 5 degrees Fahrenheit, and despite the heated cabin, the unofficial barograph froze. Fortunately the official sealed unit continued to operate accurately. She could barely read the official instrument through the viewing window, but by the time she thought it read 24,000 feet and the outside temperature reached minus 15 degrees, Marvel decided to head back down. Even with supplemental oxygen she had started to become lightheaded and was worried she might lose control of the plane.

When Marvel brought the Ryan back to earth, she had been in the air for two hours and twelve minutes. When the barograph was unsealed and read in Washington, D.C., Marvel officially held a new altitude record at 23,996 feet. She had broken the old record by more than 3,700 feet!

Marvel was the talk of the nation. She appeared in newsreels and on the cover of New York Mid-Week Pictorial, which dubbed her the "New Star of the Clouds." She was featured in Ryan Aircraft advertisements in *Time* magazine alongside Charles Lindbergh. Her image promoted Union Oil and Oldsmobile automobiles. At the height of her fame, Marvel again turned to racing. She was the first entrant in the longest air race ever created for women.

~

THE FIRST WOMEN'S Air Derby was scheduled for August 1929. Dubbed the Powder Puff Derby, the race featured twenty of the best-qualified women pilots in the world, competing for more than $15,000 in prize money. From the United States came Amelia Earhart, Bobbie Trout, Ruth Elder, Florence "Poncho" Barnes, Louise Thaden, and more than a dozen others. Also racing were Thea Rasch of Germany and Mrs. Keith Miller of New Zealand. Marvel Crosson, at the age of twenty-nine, was the youngest to enter, but she was considered by many to be the most experienced pilot in the race.

Marvel needed a fast plane to compete and one of the best was offered. Walter Beech offered Marvel a sleek new open-cockpit Travel Air Speedwing Chaparral made by his Kansas company. She excitedly wired her brother Joe, who was in New York, and asked him to meet her in Wichita to look at the plane. Marvel also told Joe she had heard from Ben Eielson, who wanted Joe to join him in Alaska as chief pilot for the new Alaskan Airways.

When the barograph was unsealed and read in Washington, D.C., Marvel officially held a new altitude record at 23,996 feet. She had broken the old record by more than 3,700 feet!

◄ *Marvel Crosson is in her full flight suit as she visits with her sister Zelma, mother Elizabeth, and father Esler before the start of the Women's Air Derby race at Santa Monica, California, on August 18, 1929.*

The official starter's pistol was fired by Cliff Henderson, who was 2,800 miles away in Cleveland. The sound of the pistol shot was carried live over the NBC radio network throughout the United States.

The flying Crossons met in Wichita in mid-July to try out the new craft and take it to Santa Monica. During one of the landings, it ground looped—swerved on the runway to one side and spun in a circle—but Marvel and Joe both liked the fast, sleek new plane. Marvel's pilot friend Emory Bronte also flew the plane and said he didn't trust it. Joe left Santa Monica and flew a good portion of the race course, planning to meet his sister at the finish line in Cleveland.

Starting at Santa Monica Municipal Airport on Sunday, August 18, 1929, the Women's Air Derby competitors would race from point to point on eight consecutive days, totaling 2,800 miles. With refueling or overnight stops in California, Arizona, New Mexico, Texas, Oklahoma, Kansas, Missouri, Illinois, and Indiana, they were scheduled to arrive in Cleveland, Ohio, in front of the crowds at the start of the National Air Races on August 26.

Rules for the race were simple. Each pilot must fly alone and pick her way across the southwestern deserts and the long, flat stretches of the Midwest. Each carried her own map, relying on her own ability to navigate the course; the planes at that time did not have two-way radios. The day before the race was a busy time for the contestants. On race day, every detail was gone over by the pilots, and their mechanics were busy tuning the engines, adjusting wires and cables, and making sure the planes were in top condition.

Hundreds of spectators lined the field for the start of the race on the bright afternoon of August 18. Contestants had arrived throughout the morning and lined up their planes for the 2:15 p.m. start. Marvel strapped on her parachute, waved at her fans, kissed her mother good-bye, and climbed in the cockpit to wait for the start signal. The official starter's pistol was fired by Cliff Henderson, who was 2,800 miles away in Cleveland. The sound of the pistol shot was carried live over the NBC radio network throughout the United States. When the shot echoed through the loudspeakers, Marvel started the engine of her sleek Travel Air and took off on the first short hop to San Bernardino.

Other contestants followed in one-minute intervals. Many pilots were worried when they saw Marvel's ship. It was clearly the fastest. Contestant Louise Thaden remembered the Travel Air:

Marvel Crosson's plane was the first flown. Her brother Joe came up to get it. The fastest of the lot, a clipped wing single seater with one of the new Wright J-6 "7" engines, it was clocked at 168 miles an hour, a discouraging factor for the rest of us. The heady glow of racing competition dimmed. A hundred and sixty-eight miles an hour! Marvel had the race cinched!

The clipped-wing craft traded stability for speed. Shorter wings allowed it to fly faster, but it was also trickier to fly and required higher takeoff and landing speeds. Marvel felt up to the challenge. During her flying career, Marvel had learned firsthand about danger. Before she went to Alaska, she had told reporters about an engine failure in the Jenny that she and Joe had rebuilt. The engine failed over the ocean, twenty-five miles from San Diego. Marvel dove the plane toward the sea in a desperate attempt to restart the motor. The plane picked up speed, the propeller started to turn again, and the old OX-5 engine roared back to life.

"The fastest of the lot . . . it was clocked at 168 miles an hour, a discouraging factor for the rest of us. The heady glow of racing competition dimmed. A hundred and sixty-eight miles an hour! Marvel had the race cinched!"

MARVEL FLEW TO San Bernardino in good time. Problems facing the other race contestants were minor. One pilot, Mabelle Waters, withdrew prior to the start and another, Mary E. Von Mach, landed at Montebello, California, with engine trouble. Amelia Earhart was temporarily delayed with starter trouble. Von Mach and Earhart arrived in San Bernardino late. Opal Kinty ground-looped while landing on the dusty strip, but damage was minor and her plane was ready to go in the morning.

Marvel awoke early the next day, thinking about the race. The course for day two crossed over remote desert and mountains and continued into Arizona. In effect, this part of the race was in her backyard. She knew the country and knew she had the fastest plane. Still she had to be on her toes. The Travel Air engine had been a bit cantankerous prior to the race. Walter Beech had sent another motor to Santa Monica, but for reasons that remain unknown, it was not installed. Her mechanics apparently felt the original problem was fixed, so Marvel took off.

On the first leg, to San Bernardino, the motor had developed trouble again. Other flyers encouraged Marvel to withdraw, but she refused. The problems didn't seem too serious. She planned to have the motor worked on in Phoenix, Arizona, at the end of the second day.

Thea Rasch had received a telegram before the race, warning of sabotage. The incident prompted rumors to spread among the racers. Race officials took the report seriously and asked local officials at each of the destination airports to monitor the flyers and their planes for safety. Marvel planned to be extra careful in her preflight checks.

In the early light of August 19, engines coughed to life and all were ready for the 6:00 a.m. departure. The racers took off one at a time from San Bernardino and climbed into the morning air. First stop was to be Yuma, Arizona, where the flyers expected the trickiest landing of the race.

It was not a trouble-free day. Thea Rasch's engine quit suddenly and her landing gear was damaged in a forced landing. She reported finding sand in her fuel tank. Bobbie Trout also damaged her gear in a forced landing, but both flyers were able to continue the race. Claire Fahy was not so lucky. Some of the wires on her craft had snapped, and she believed someone had poured acid on them. She was out of the race.

At Yuma, heat waves radiating from the ground and drifting sand made the runway difficult to see. Marvel found the airstrip and landed safely. She didn't report any more motor trouble and continued on after refueling. While landing at Yuma, Amelia Earhart nosed over and damaged her plane's propeller. A new one was flown out from Los Angeles and she continued the race.

In spite of the mishaps during the day, the remaining contestants straggled into Phoenix. People were concerned when Marvel's plane didn't arrive when it was expected. By nightfall of August 19, the remaining flyers had landed safely, except for one. Marvel Crosson was missing.

All that the other contestants could do was hope and pray for Marvel's safety. She was well-respected by her peers, and camaraderie among the elite group of pilots was strong. They left Phoenix the next day without knowing her fate, but confident that Marvel could handle herself in any difficult flying situation.

Ranchers along the Gila River near Wellton, Arizona, were the first to report seeing a plane go down in a remote area of the mountains. Local searchers organized and scoured the mountains and valleys in the cool evening air. Plans were made in Phoenix and Los Angeles to send search planes in the morning. They weren't needed. At seven o'clock in the morning of August 20, searchers from Wellton found the Travel Air crashed in a ravine. Marvel was dead.

The beautiful, good-natured "star of the clouds" was gone. Her body was in a crumpled heap, lying on her parachute. The Travel Air had hit nose first. Marvel had bailed out of the plane and pulled the

◄ *Ten of the Women's Air Derby contestants pose before the race with trophies to be awarded after the competition. The flyers (left to right) are Louise Thaden, Bobbie Trout, Patty Willis, Marvel Crosson, Blanche Noyes, Vera Walker, Amelia Earhart, Marjorie Crawford, Ruth Elder, and Florence "Pancho" Barnes.*

"Women pilots were blazing a new trail. Each pioneering effort must bow to death. There has never been nor will there ever be progress without sacrifice of human life."

ripcord on the parachute, but it had not fully opened. Pilots who visited the scene said she was probably flying too low for the chute to have saved her life. Her broken watch was stopped at 12:16. A hundred feet away the smashed clock in the Travel Air also read 12:16. The plane hit the ground with such impact that four of the seven cylinders were torn from the motor.

The searchers carefully wrapped Marvel's body in the silken folds of her parachute. Her body was taken by ambulance to Yuma and flown back to California for burial. The Crosson family, the Women's Air Derby contestants, and the nation was stunned. Stories of possible sabotage abounded, and others recounted Marvel's problems with the engine. Walter Beech confirmed the engine problems and couldn't explain why the new motor had not been installed.

Nowhere was the shock greater than with Joe Crosson at the finish line. His sister, friend, and partner was gone. He knew he had to get to San Diego to be with his family, but no scheduled flights were available from Cleveland. He recognized one of the planes on the line as belonging to a friend. With a sense of urgency fueled by his grief, he took the plane and flew to Chicago to catch a flight to the West Coast, without first securing permission from the plane's owner.

The other racers were devastated. They had landed in Douglas, Arizona, hoping to hear that Marvel was back in the competition, but instead learned of her death. A dark cloud shrouded the air derby. Newspapers called for the race to be canceled, but many people believed that Marvel would want it to continue. The pilots and others closest to Marvel knew it must go on. So the race continued. Race winner Louise Thaden shared her own feelings:

If your time has come to go, it is a glorious way in which to pass over. . . . Women pilots were blazing a new trail. Each pioneering effort must bow to death. There has never been nor will there ever be progress without sacrifice of human life.

Marvel's death was tragic, but she knew the risks. Earlier she wrote a letter to a grieving mother who had lost two daughters in an air accident, saying, "Don't worry; every flyer would rather go with her plane instead of a more lingering way. Just think of the thrill of making immediate contact with the spiritual while doing the thing one loves to do most."

Although she felt the grief of losing a daughter, Elizabeth Crosson believed Marvel had lived a longer and fuller life in her short years than most people live in a hundred. Echoing her daughter's sentiments, Elizabeth said, "Marvel died just as she wanted to go—in an airplane."

There was someone else who shared in the grief. Since their first meeting, Marvel and Emory Bronte had become very close. They were planning to be married in Cleveland after the Women's Air Derby. A note found in Marvel's belongings said:

Sweetheart:
    Goodbye and good luck. I know everything will be alright and that you are going to win. Will be with you every minute and waiting for you at Cleveland.

                        Love, Emory

The day following the crash, a magazine article Marvel had written appeared on newsstands. In it she wrote, "I have given up my life to prove women are the best pilots in the world."

Echoing her daughter's sentiments, Elizabeth said, "Marvel died just as she wanted to go—in an airplane."

Joe with Waco 10

10

TRAGEDY IN SIBERIA

Fairbanks, autumn 1929. Joe Crosson returned to Alaska with a heavy heart. Marvel was gone. Now he carried on alone the dream of flying they had shared since that day at the dusty Colorado fairground so long ago. Each time he headed skyward he felt closer to Marvel. Flying was a way he could continue to spend time with her in the clear, crisp air over Alaska. The new business venture with his friend, Ben Eielson, gave him that chance.

Crosson was headed back to a job that would most certainly keep him in the air. He was chief pilot of Alaskan Airways, based in Fairbanks. With financial backing from the Delaware-based Aviation Corporation of America (parent company of American Airways, later to be known as American Airlines), Alaskan Airways had purchased the planes and facilities of Wien Alaska Airways in Nome, the Bennett-Rodebaugh Company in Fairbanks, and Anchorage Air Transport.

Pilots from the three companies now flew for Alaskan Airways, which was a subsidiary of American Airways, and Joe was their leader. Eielson, who was older and more experienced than Joe, was general manager and pilot.

Marvel's memory weighed heavily on Joe but events of the day left little time to think about personal loss. Stepping off the boat in the

August 8-29, 1929
The Graf Zeppelin makes the first airship round-the-world flight, starting and finishing at Lakehurst, New Jersey.

◄ *Joe braved bitter cold flying the open-cockpit Waco 10 during the search for Ben Eielson.*

Before being rescued,
Merrill had trekked
alone over the tundra
for eleven long days
and kept himself alive
by eating raw lemmings
he shot with his pistol.

salty coastal air at Seward, he received bad news. Russ Merrill, a fellow Alaskan Airways pilot, was missing and Joe was needed immediately to join the search.

Merrill was last seen the evening of September 16 when he loaded a Travel Air floatplane with mining machinery and mail and departed for Bear Creek on the Kuskokwim River, northwest of Anchorage. Merrill vanished five days before Crosson returned to Alaska.

The searchers had reason for hope. It was not unusual for pilots to land and wait out bad weather or deal with equipment problems that occurred during flights. Like Crosson, Merrill was an outdoorsman capable of surviving in the wild for weeks at a time. A few months earlier Merrill had landed on a frozen arctic lake on wheels to wait out an early snowstorm but was unable to take off in the newly fallen snow. Before being rescued, Merrill had trekked alone over the tundra for eleven long days and kept himself alive by eating raw lemmings he shot with his pistol. If Merrill was forced down on the flight to Bear Creek, he could survive.

Short delays were not uncommon, but if pilots failed to return after a few days a serious search was mounted. In this case, searchers held out hope that Merrill was simply stranded. With no aircraft radios, no phone or telegraph service in the bush, and Army Signal Corps communication radios scattered hundreds of miles apart, he would have had no way to get a message back to Anchorage.

When a pilot was missing, routine air travel was kept to a minimum while most available pilots joined the search. Crosson took the train from Seward to Anchorage, where Ben Eielson picked him up and filled him in on details of the search. Crosson immediately went to work putting floats on another Alaskan Airways Travel Air. He tightened the last bolt, stowed his tools, and took off.

Flying out of Anchorage, pilots searched tirelessly throughout the region for a month. Looking down on vast forests, rivers, lakes, mountains, and Cook Inlet, eyes strained to catch a glimpse of the stranded Travel Air. Crosson's trips covered hundreds of miles ranging southwest to Seldovia, across Kachemak Bay, and northwest to Iditarod in the rolling Interior. As time wore on, chances that Merrill was safe

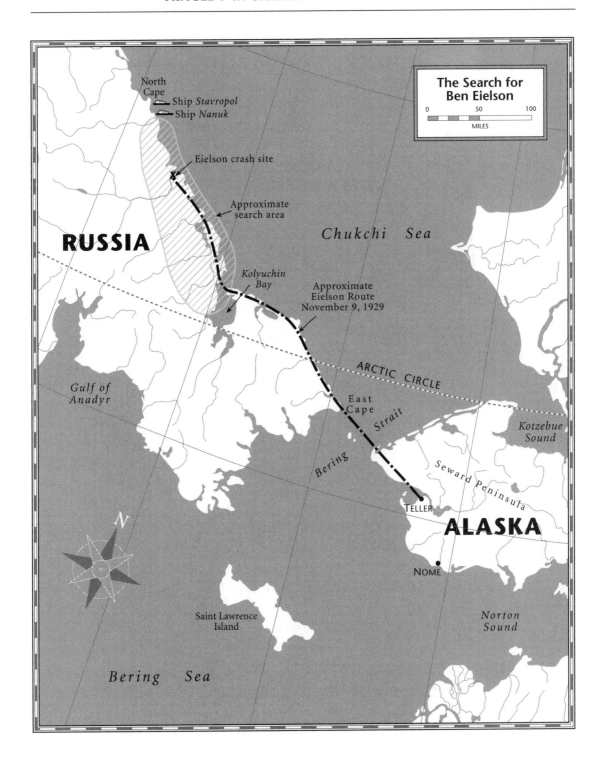

The Search for
Ben Eielson

0   50   100

MILES

North
Cape
Ship *Stavropol*
Ship *Nanuk*

Eielson crash site

Approximate
search area

Chukchi   Sea

RUSSIA

*Kolyuchin
Bay*

Approximate
Eielson Route
November 9, 1929

ARCTIC CIRCLE

*Gulf of
Anadyr*

East
Cape

Kotzebue
Sound

Bering   Strait

Seward Peninsula

TELLER

ALASKA

NOME

Saint Lawrence
Island

*Norton
Sound*

Bering   Sea

▲ Harold Gillam, who had earned his pilot's license only the previous summer, flew a Stearman C2B to support Joe Crosson in the search for Ben Eielson.

diminished and hopes faded. Searching continued until heavy snow blanketed the region in mid-October.

A few days later, Russ Merrill's fate was known. The owner of a fish trap across Cook Inlet from Anchorage arrived in town with a yard-long piece of stitched green fabric that had been caught in his trap. It was identified as a piece of the plane Merrill was flying, by the mechanic who installed it earlier in the year. Another year passed before a strip of wood with an aircraft banking level identified as a part of Merrill's plane was found on a Cook Inlet beach. Russ Merrill's luck had run out.

After the tiring search, Crosson returned to Fairbanks just as the town settled into the long, cold, dark winter. Keeping a cabin warm all day long with a woodstove was nearly impossible for single people who worked for a living. As a result, many young people who could afford it lived in the Nordale Hotel during the cold season. Crosson took a room in the Nordale, and one day he bumped into the pretty young lady from Cordova who had been such a good friend of Marvel's.

Joe asked Lillian Osborne out to a show at the Empress Theatre. As Joe bought tickets, theater manager (and piano player) Don Adler came out and suggested that the young couple take a walk before the movie, which wouldn't begin for a little while. Adler had a reason for sending the couple off on a walk before the featured film. Joe and Lillian later found out that the newsreel that evening, screened before the movie, featured Marvel's accident and death.

Joe and Lillian began seeing each other and were soon a regular couple at community dances and other social events. They sometimes double-dated with Ben Eielson and Marie Banks, a schoolteacher he was seeing at the time.

Joe and Lillian later found out that the newsreel that evening, screened before the movie, featured Marvel's accident and death.

~

DESPITE THE TRAGIC loss of Russ Merrill, things looked good for Alaskan Airways. The airline already had the most experienced pilots and best equipment in the Territory. The next step was to pursue business.

A unique opportunity arrived in November. Trader Olaf Swenson, who made a living trading supplies and equipment in Siberia for fur pelts, contacted Eielson. Swenson was aboard the stranded schooner *Nanuk*, which was trapped in the arctic ice off the coast of Siberia and frozen in for the winter. The schooner's cargo of fur pelts was worth more than a million dollars back in the United States, and Swenson was willing to pay well to get the pelts and most of the crew back to Alaska right away. In spite of the remoteness of the region in Siberia, high above the Arctic Circle, Eielson took the chance. Success would greatly help the new aviation company.

Weather off North Cape in Siberia's Arctic is treacherous; storms and blizzards often last for weeks. It was risky, but there was precedence for attempting the flights. Less than a year earlier, Noel Wien made one trip to another of Swenson's ships, the *Elisif*, which like the *Nanuk* had frozen in the ice with a load of furs. Wien would have gone back, but

The Nanuk had become trapped as it raced to the ice-free waters of the south, and Swenson faced financial ruin if he were to lose two ships within a year.

the Soviet government had denied permission for additional flights. The *Elisif* was eventually lost to the cruel Arctic.

The *Nanuk* had become trapped as it raced to the ice-free waters of the south, and Swenson faced financial ruin if he were to lose two ships within a year. Coincidentally, the *Stavropol*, a Russian steamer that had joined the *Nanuk* in the race to get away from the winter ice, was also caught and frozen fast. The ships were within sight of each other.

Swenson was able to communicate with the outside world via radio using Morse code. Swenson and Alaskan Airways made arrangements, and the Soviet government granted permission, for a series of flights from Alaska to Siberia. Leaving Crosson in charge of routine flying out of Fairbanks, Eielson and one of his pilots, Frank Dorbandt, flew two planes to Teller, on the western Alaska coast near Nome.

"Clear skies and no wind at the *Nanuk*" was the message transmitted October 29 by young radioman Bob Gleason from on board the schooner. In Teller, 450 miles away, Eielson received the message. Similar weather conditions in Teller encouraged him to try the flight.

Eielson was delayed with equipment problems at Teller. But Dorbandt, flying a Stinson Detroiter, was able to reach the *Nanuk* and land, making the cold flight in just over six hours. The crew welcomed mail and coffee from Alaska. Most of the cargo space in the plane was filled with cans of aviation gas for the upcoming flights from the *Nanuk*. Eielson and mechanic Earl Borland arrived the following afternoon in their Hamilton aircraft.

The stranded ship's crew and their rescuers spent an enjoyable evening on the *Nanuk*. Captain R. H. Weeding's crew included twelve men, plus Swenson and Swenson's seventeen-year-old daughter Marion. Warmed by the coal stove, the crew looked forward to the hot baths and other amenities that waited back in Alaska. The twenty-three-year-old radioman, Gleason, remembered that the good-natured Eielson, a former schoolteacher, challenged all aboard to a spelling contest. Gleason won by spelling eight of ten words correctly.

The morning weather deteriorated as the first passengers and furs

were loaded in the planes. The pilots ran into heavy snow, and both planes landed near a Siberian Chukchi village to wait out the storm. Winds howled for four days as the travelers waited in Native huts. Finally the skies cleared. The pilots heated motors, loaded passengers, and took off. Both planes landed safely in Alaska by dark.

The weather now turned ugly both at Teller and the *Nanuk*. Another four days passed. When Gleason reported passable weather at the *Nanuk* on November 9, the two planes lifted into clear skies from Teller. Dorbandt soon returned to Teller, reporting heavy fog over the Bering Strait, but Eielson and Borland pressed on into the gloom. By evening, the big Hamilton had neither arrived at the *Nanuk* nor returned to Teller. Several days later good weather returned, but still no word came about the plane's whereabouts. Ben Eielson, the famous arctic flyer, was missing. It was the beginning of a long, heavy winter.

▲ *Pilot Ed Young (left), mechanic Herb Larison, and Joe Crosson prepare a load of supplies in Teller for a flight to the Nanuk. Cargo includes cans of aviation gas, plus propeller blades wrapped in burlap that were used to repair airplanes damaged during the Eielson search.*

He held Lillian close and kissed her, then looked deep into her eyes and said, "I won't come back until I find Ben."

Hundreds of square miles of arctic bleakness lay between Teller and the *Nanuk*. There were no clues to Eielson's location. In mid-November, when Chukchi Natives arrived at the *Nanuk*, they told of seeing a plane near their village the day Eielson left Teller. Then a Russian trapper just fifty miles from the *Nanuk* reported hearing a plane heading inland on the same day. On November 23, Olaf Swenson organized a search. Two dog teams were sent inland to look for Eielson. The Russian government contributed two airplanes that were loaded on an icebreaking ship headed north to assist the *Stavropol*. Again, Alaskan Airways dropped back to minimum service to allow pilots to help search. This time it was their leader, Ben Eielson, who was missing.

Pilots were outdoorsmen who could take care of themselves in the wilds, and people didn't panic when they failed to arrive on schedule. Searches were usually organized within a week or so of when they disappeared. In this case, weather and equipment challenges delayed the search even longer.

Between flights out of Fairbanks, Crosson heard that Eielson was missing. He planned to leave home to search for him, but couldn't go without saying good-bye to Lillian. He and Lillian had become very close. Before he left, he called on her and they talked quite a while. He held Lillian close and kissed her, then looked deep into her eyes and said, "I won't come back until I find Ben."

"That was it," Lillian later recalled. "I knew he meant it. He was a very determined man."

~

CROSSON WAS THE first of the search pilots to reach Teller, in an open-cockpit Waco on November 29. Dorbandt had experienced engine trouble at Teller and did not return to the *Nanuk* or join the search.

The *Nanuk* was stranded off an undeveloped part of Siberia with no towns or landing strips. Only three pilots in Alaska had the experience to take arctic winter flying challenges in stride. Noel Wien was out of the Territory, and Ben Eielson was missing. Joe Crosson was the other.

Flying conditions were nearly impossible. The midwinter sun ventures above the horizon for mere minutes a day above the Arctic Circle, if at all. When treacherous weather did allow planes to fly, thousands of square miles of darkness awaited searchers. Maintaining airplanes was a constant challenge. All of the difficulties of preheating motors and oil were intensified in the bitter Siberian cold. Wings had to be covered and skis blocked up each time the planes stopped so they wouldn't freeze to the ice. Jagged ice on an improvised runway at the *Nanuk* damaged more than one plane. Weather predictions were unavailable, maps were crude, and airplanes did not carry radios.

The only communication the searchers had was from the *Nanuk*. Radioman Gleason could send messages to Teller, and from there they could be relayed to Nome and Barrow and eventually reach the outside world. Geography also complicated communications. The international dateline runs between Siberia and Alaska, so messages dated from the *Nanuk* arrived on the previous date in Alaska.

Gleason also sent personal messages from pilots and crew at the *Nanuk* to loved ones far away. More than once, Crosson filed wires to Lillian so she wouldn't worry.

Alaskan Airways dedicated as many planes as possible to the search effort, even though most of its fleet was open-cockpit and poorly suited for flying in the bitter cold. By the end of November several pilots waited out bad weather in Teller with Crosson.

Eielson was a hero and his whereabouts was important news. Swenson wired updates about the search from the *Nanuk* to Teller, where it was relayed to the rest of the world. Newspapers across the continent carried daily stories about the lost flyers, which generated more support for the search.

The backers for Alaskan Airways, the Aviation Corporation of America, sent three new Fairchild 71 cabin monoplanes with pilots to join the search in December. Two Fairchilds were shipped to Seattle via rail from Chicago and Winnipeg. One flew to Seattle from Los Angeles. From Seattle they were shipped on a Coast Guard cutter to Seward. Alaska's governor arranged for a special train to take them to Fairbanks, where they were reassembled.

Flying conditions were nearly impossible. The midwinter sun ventures above the horizon for mere minutes a day above the Arctic Circle, if at all. When treacherous weather did allow planes to fly, thousands of square miles of darkness awaited searchers.

The oil burned for several hours, but no planes came. The next daylight came about ten o'clock the following morning. The day wore on, but still no planes.

Meantime, it was up to the planes and pilots of Alaskan Airways. Planes left Teller several times trying to fly to the *Nanuk*. Each time, they were turned back by midwinter darkness and stormy weather. At 9:30 a.m. on December 20, Crosson in a Waco and pilot Harold Gillam in a Stearman flew out of Teller. In the arctic twilight they endured minus-20-degree cold in their open cockpits while flying toward Siberia. Each plane carried a sleeping bag, a plumber's pot for warming the motor, a month's food rations, and sixty-five gallons of gas in five-gallon cans.

Aboard the *Nanuk*, Gleason received the message that Crosson and Gillam were on their way, so the ship's crew marked out a rough ice runway with barrels. They burned oil in the barrels to mark the runway after dark. The oil burned for several hours, but no planes came. The next daylight came about ten o'clock the following morning. The day wore on, but still no planes. As darkness again overtook the stranded vessel, one lone craft approached and landed.

Harold Gillam climbed stiffly out of the Stearman and recounted his flight. He and Crosson encountered bad weather the previous afternoon. In the foggy darkness Crosson picked a spot on the ice and landed, followed closely by Gillam. They were near a Chukchi Native village and spent the night with the generous residents of a hut. Crosson and Gillam talked over the hazardous weather and the challenges they faced. They agreed that if they became separated during the flight the next day, they would return to the village.

After warming the planes in the early-morning darkness, they were off again for the *Nanuk* in temperatures that dropped to 35 degrees below zero Fahrenheit. Within minutes, thick fog surrounded them, and the planes separated. Crosson immediately began searching for Gillam. Crosson felt responsible for him. The previous year in Fairbanks, Marvel had encouraged Gillam to take up flying and invited him to stay with Esler and Elizabeth Crosson in San Diego while taking lessons. Gillam had logged fewer than fifty hours total flying time and had received his license only that summer.

Crosson eventually returned to the Native village, as agreed. But Gillam pressed on. Incredible luck rode with him: he narrowly avoided crashing into a hillside and he managed to find the *Nanuk*.

Light was minimal when Crosson arrived back over the village. His goggles frosted up in the fog, and in spite of the bitter cold he had to push them up on his leather helmet and peer around the frosty windshield to see where to land. His face was in the slipstream for only a minute—long enough to frost the corneas of his eyes.

Before the night was over, worry and fear combined to nearly overwhelm the young pilot. As Crosson sat in the hut before a flickering fire, he worried about Gillam and whether he had crashed in the fog. He thought about his friend Eielson and wondered whether he could still be alive. Pain from the injury to his eyes was intense. Crosson wasn't sure how he could contact the other pilots or searchers from the village, where no one spoke English. It was a long and troubling night.

Crosson stared at the fire for hours, seeing circles around the flames. Toward dawn he realized the rings were getting larger, and his vision was improving. He still didn't know what had happened to Gillam, but he knew he would be able to keep searching—maybe for both Eielson and Gillam. By morning he was able to see well enough to fly again.

The following morning Harold Gillam was preheating the Stearman when Crosson's plane arrived at the *Nanuk*. Crosson was cold and exhausted from his sleepless night in the Native hut, but he climbed out of the Waco and rushed to give Gillam a big bear hug.

Leaving Crosson to rest, Gillam and Swenson flew off to search an area in the foothills where the Chukchi Eskimos had heard the plane. No trace was found, and they returned to the *Nanuk*. Roused by the Stearman landing next to the ship and a brief report from Gillam, Crosson headed for the radio room of the *Nanuk*. In the dimly lit room, Bob Gleason keyed Crosson's message to Alfred Lomen in Nome, who was coordinating search efforts on the Alaska side of the Bering Strait for the Aviation Corporation. The telegram kept to business and only hinted at the relief Joe felt:

Lomen, Nome – December 21, 1929
    Arrived here today okay – Lost Gillam yesterday – After

Joe's goggles frosted up in the fog, and in spite of the bitter cold he had to push them up on his leather helmet and peer around the frosty windshield to see where to land. His face was in the slipstream for only a minute—long enough to frost the corneas of his eyes.

Despite Crosson's vast experience and skill, he could manage only one search flight before Christmas. Again, no sign of the missing airmen.

looking around for him went back to Native village where we stayed night before – Glad he arrived okay yesterday – Gillam and Swenson out two hours twenty minutes – Saw nothing searching back of Lagoon – Will use up what gas we have here for search – Then will have to wait for other ships.

Joe Crosson – North Cape, Siberia

Weather conditions deteriorated. The amount of daylight shortened each day until the sun failed to break the horizon at all. Searching in the dark, bleak, bitterly cold region became increasingly difficult. Despite Crosson's vast experience and skill, he could manage only one search flight before Christmas. Again, no sign of the missing airmen. Limited stores of aviation gas were supplemented with low-grade gas from the *Stavropol*. Another severe storm nearly halted the search altogether. Christmas passed with little cheer at the stranded ship.

Now, six weeks after they vanished, chances of finding Eielson and Borland alive were remote, but Crosson kept trying. When the storm broke, Crosson and Gillam preheated the motors of their planes and took off. Bitter cold and low-octane fuel conspired against them. Gillam's motor faltered just after he became airborne and the Stearman landed hard on the ice just behind the *Nanuk*. A wing panel and wing support were damaged and both gear struts were broken. Crosson managed only two short search flights while Gillam's forlorn craft was being repaired where it sat on the ice. Crosson's telegrams to Lomen in Nome tell the story:

Lomen, Nome – December 29, 1929

Unable fly since twenty sixth account blizzard – Cleared up some today – Harold damaged landing gear when engine quit after taking off – Sending dog team in morning to Deer Camp back of lagoon – The vicinity where Eielson last heard has been well covered and if he went inland must have been heard near Deer Camps – Anxious to get in touch with them – Impossible land near camps so necessary send dog teams.

Crosson – North Cape, Siberia

Lomen, Nome – December 30, 1929

Storm continues here today – Impossible dog teams start – Everyone here giving all possible assistance – Will continue search with plane when weather and visibility favorable.

Crosson – North Cape, Siberia

There was no New Year's celebration for the pilots and staff of Alaskan Airways in 1930. All attention was focused on Siberia and the whereabouts of their founder, Ben Eielson. Logistics for the search were not going smoothly. Supplies were being ferried by air from Fairbanks to Teller for the search, but one of the three Fairchild airplanes shipped from Seattle crashed in the bitter cold just after takeoff from Fairbanks and was extensively damaged. Canadian pilot Pat Reid was forced to land a second Fairchild in a remote mountain streambed near Nulato when he became lost, and it took a week to improvise repairs that permitted the plane to take off again. Only one of the three original Fairchilds made it to Nome unscathed.

Telegrams from Joe Crosson at the *Nanuk* detailed the aviators' plight there:

Lomen, Nome – January 4, 1930

Wind changed to Northwest this morning blowing real blizzard now – Teams did not return may be held up until storm subsides – Native from fifty miles Southwest North Cape came in and reports no planes heard that direction – Will have information concerning Wrangell weather reports tomorrow – Stavrapol is equipping expedition to start searching country adjacent to coast between North Cape and Serge – Natives arriving from Westward have not heard any planes.

Joe – North Cape, Siberia

Lomen, Nome – January 5, 1930

Having worst storm of winter – Will be impossible go Stavrapol …

Joe – North Cape, Siberia

Supplies were being ferried by air from Fairbanks to Teller for the search, but . . . only one of the three original Fairchilds made it to Nome unscathed.

I could see something that looked like a wing— this was actually the shadow of the left wing on the snow . . . It would have been impossible to pick this out had the sun not been shining.

Lomen, Nome – January 8, 1930
    Impossible flying weather today . . .

Joe – North Cape, Siberia

Periods of improving weather were brief, and the only searches started during the month were by mushers with dog teams.

The sun finally broke the horizon at the *Nanuk* again on January 26, and the weather improved. Crosson took off in the Waco. Gillam in the repaired Stearman joined him and they headed south to search an area near where Chukchi Eskimos and a trader had reported hearing a plane November 9. The pilots agreed to maintain a steady distance between the planes, and if one of them sighted something he would wag his wings to signal the other.

Late in the day the Waco and the Stearman returned and taxied up to the *Nanuk*. Crosson got out. "The search is over," he said. "We found the plane."

Crosson somberly walked to the radio room on the *Nanuk* and sent the long-awaited and dreaded message to Ben Eielson's father in North Dakota. (Due to the international dateline, the telegram was dated a day earlier.)

Eielson, Hatton, North Dakota – January 25, 1930
    Regret to inform you found Ben's plane badly wrecked about ninety miles east here – Plane buried in deep snow did not locate bodies - Very evident killed instantly – Pilots cockpit torn away with engine which lies about hundred feet from cabin – dispatching dog teams to excavate snow around plane

Joe Crosson – North Cape, Siberia

In due course Crosson told the *Nanuk* crew about finding the missing plane:

Flying about a thousand feet high a few miles back of the beach line, I saw a black object on the white snow. This area had been thoroughly covered by planes and dogteams and I nearly passed it

up but decided to go down and take a closer look. Upon turning towards the object, I could see something that looked like a wing—this was actually the shadow of the left wing on the snow. When within about 200 feet, I could distinguish the wing of the plane. It would have been impossible to pick this out had the sun not been shining.

Crosson signaled to Gillam that he would land. Gillam followed and both pilots climbed out to inspect the crash site.

Eielson's plane had suffered tremendous damage, and it was clear no one could have survived. Debris was scattered over several hundred feet, with the right wing lying two hundred feet from the main fuselage. The landing gear and cabin were demolished, and the motor was torn completely off. Although the wreck was only about fifty feet above sea level, the altimeter indicated one thousand feet. The throttle was wide open and the propeller was wrapped around the engine, which had several cylinders broken off. Eielson obviously had not been attempting to land. There was no sign of the bodies of Eielson and Borland. Crosson and Gillam spent two hours at the site before returning to the *Nanuk*.

▲ *A wing of the crashed Hamilton aircraft of Ben Eielson rises above the Siberian snows. A shadow cast by the wing caught Joe Crosson's attention while he searched for his missing friend and fellow pilot. After landing at the site, Crosson could tell no one had survived.*

Workers from the
Stavropol joined the
others as the searchers
dug a series of trenches
over the next several
days, searching for
the bodies.

Crosson was put in charge of the American and Canadian efforts to coordinate flights in Siberia and find the bodies. Radioman Bob Gleason was impressed by Crosson's natural leadership: "Quietly, calmly, and without direct orders, he kept pilots, mechanics, Americans, Canadians and Russians working together to complete the search." Workers from the *Stavropol* joined the others as the searchers dug a series of trenches over the next several days, searching for the bodies.

Crosson was surprised and touched by a telegram he received back at the *Nanuk* from Ben Eielson's father.

> Crosson, MS *Nanuk* – January 29 1930
> Knew that if my son was found you would be the one to do it –
> Hope to be able tell you personally of my indebtedness to you

when I arrive in Alaska next month – Please thank Gillam and all others for me who aided in the search and tell them of my heartfelt appreciation of their work.

O. E. Eielson – Hatton, North Dakota

Another, shorter telegram inspired him for the future:

Crosson, *Nanuk* – February 1 1930
Sorry about Ben – Anxiously waiting your return

Love Lillian – Fairbanks

At the site of the wreckage the search continued, but not without further complications. Two Russian Junkers airplanes landed at the

◄ *Russian sailors dig trenches at the crash site, searching for the bodies of Eielson and Borland. The Russians came from the steamer* Stavropol, *which was frozen in for the winter.*

▲ A snow shelter was built under the wing of a Russian Junkers airplane for diggers at the crash site.

Nanuk on January 29. One pilot misjudged the ice runway, running onto snowdrifts past the end and damaging the landing gear. The planes were originally sent by the Soviets to carry out the *Stavropol* passengers, but the news of Crosson's find brought orders from Moscow to join the search for the dead airmen. Russian pilot Marikia Slepnev flew his Junkers to Eielson's crash site and landed without mishap. The plane provided shelter for the searchers, who built a snow house around part of the plane, with the wing serving as a roof.

Meanwhile, Joe remained busy organizing searchers and shuttling people between the *Nanuk* and the crash site. With gas supplies critically low, Canadian pilot Pat Reid carried a load of aviation gas from Teller and attempted to land at the site in one of the new Fairchilds. He misjudged the surface and tore off the landing gear. Jim Hutchison was sent from Teller to start repairs on the crippled craft.

Digging for the bodies continued between fierce blizzards that refused to let up. Crosson wired as each new clue was found: first Borland's flying helmet and mittens, then the pilot's seat, then Eielson's flying helmet. Finally, after a labyrinth of trenches had been dug in search of the airmen, Borland's body was located on February 16.

Two days later Joe again wired Nome.

Lomen, Nome February 19 1930
    Ben's body found on eighteenth – bodies being brought north
Cape tomorrow

Crosson – North Cape, Siberia

Both men had died instantly. In an act of kindness, the Russian
women passengers on the *Stavropol* sewed American flags to cover the
fallen fliers. Permission was granted for Russian pilot Slepnev to

▲ *The bodies of Ben Eielson
and Earl Borland lie
beneath American flags
sewn by Russian women.
The men were killed in a
November 1929 crash
during a flight to the
icebound schooner* Nanuk.

▶ *Pilot Robbie Robbins (left) and Joe Crosson are pictured aboard the Nanuk in May 1930. After the bodies of Eielson and Borland were recovered, the original work of flying out furs from the stranded schooner was continued.*

accompany the bodies back to Alaska. A formation of three planes, one Russian and two from Alaska, made the flight to Fairbanks. They arrived in the bright sunshine on March 10.

The world lost a hero. Joe Crosson lost a friend. The nation had learned of the heroic efforts to locate Eielson, and of Crosson's role in the search. Alaska became even more proud of her adopted son.

An editorial in the *Seward Gateway* summed up Alaskan feelings toward Joe, praising him and "his steadfast and daring companions whose indefatigable labors battled down Arctic blizzards and braved a thousand hazards" to recover the flyers' bodies.

"It was not monetary gain that inspired his brave action," the editorial said, "nor was it a gesture for fame. It was the spirit of the air corps. . . . Already Joe Crosson has paid a terrible price for his courage—a loving sister crashed while competing in a cross country contest. Yet when the hour came for action, he faltered not. Alaska is proud to number him among its great family."

"It was not monetary gain that inspired his brave action," the editorial said, "nor was it a gesture for fame. It was the spirit of the air corps."

Lillian and Joe with Fannie Quigley

11

DOMESTICATED EAGLE

Fairbanks, summer 1930. If Joe Crosson was not the most eligible bachelor in the Territory of Alaska, he was certainly very high on the list. He was young, cheerful, handsome, and known throughout Alaska and the United States. He had traveled extensively and caught the eye of young ladies across the country. Several women fell for the dashing pilot, but the only one Joe fell for was Lillian Osborne.

Lillian knew Joe was wildly popular both within and outside the Territory, and she was very flattered by his attention. He teased her and sang parodies of popular songs to her. He even recited poetry. Lillian's beauty, grace, fiercely independent nature, and sense of humor captivated Joe. During this time, Joe's mother came to Fairbanks to visit. It may have been coincidental, but Lillian believes Mother Crosson came north to check out the young lady Joe had mentioned so many times.

Most of their friends realized how close the couple had become and were happy for them. Some people had different views. A friend of Lillian's asked her to leave Joe alone so she could have a chance to date him. One smitten young lady from Seattle sent him letters during the search for Ben Eielson and went so far as to announce that she was engaged to the pilot, which came as a big surprise to Joe. Some people

▲ *Nanuk the puppy stands in the snow. Joe brought the puppy from Siberia as a gift for his future bride.*
◄ *Joe and Lillian visit with Fannie Quigley at the Quigley mine near Kantishna.*

Lillian was working for the
F.E. Company, and her
supervisor Walter Pratt
knew how thrilled she was
when Joe would buzz the
building and wag his
wings to say hello.

in Fairbanks pressured their adopted hero to marry a local girl; they considered Lillian, who was from Cordova, to be an outsider.

When he finally popped the question, Lillian, who had grown to love his sense of humor, thought he was teasing and didn't take him seriously. The second time he proposed marriage, she believed him and excitedly agreed to become his wife.

When a couple announced their engagement in Fairbanks, they were the subject of a great deal of joking. Grant Elliot was the last pilot who had been wed there. Joe had led a group of friends in attaching an airplane rudder to the poor fellow's car, and they locked a ball and chain around Grant's leg on his wedding day. Joe knew that turnabout was fair play, and he expected the worst.

Joe and Lillian planned a honeymoon trip outside the Territory with Mother Crosson and had tickets on the steamship from Cordova. They knew that whatever spectacle their friends might plan could cause them to miss the boat. They decided to keep their marriage plans secret.

The plan was for Joe to invite Lillian along on his next commercial flight to Teller. The owner of the roadhouse there, where Joe had spent so much time waiting out storms during the search for Ben Eielson, was also a territorial commissioner and had volunteered to perform the marriage ceremony. It was just a matter of waiting for the next miner or other customer to hire Joe for a flight to Teller.

They waited in vain for a flight to Teller to materialize. But on August 3, 1930, Joe was hired to fly a man to Nenana, fifty miles southwest of Fairbanks. Lillian was working for the F.E. Company, and her supervisor Walter Pratt knew how thrilled she was when Joe would buzz the building and wag his wings to say hello. When Joe invited Lillian to ride along to Nenana, Pratt gave her time off.

The afternoon sunlight shown in the couple's eyes during the flight as the plane's motor hummed along. Aspen and birch trees were still green, but an occasional golden branch hinted that autumn was approaching.

They landed in Nenana, a river town that was kept busy by the Alaska Railroad station and a bustling business in river travel on stern-

wheelers and freight barges. Joe and Lillian walked through Nenana
and saw Volney Richmond, who, along with his new wife, ran his
father's NC Company. They didn't tell him what they were up to as
they exchanged pleasantries. The couple found Commissioner C. C.
Hyde, a pleasant woman who was fond of Joe, and she performed their
civil marriage ceremony in Nenana. Joe gave Lillian a simple gold ring,

▲ Mr. & Mrs. Joe
Crosson pose in front
of a new Ryan airplane
in San Diego during
their honeymoon in
the summer of 1930.

She asked her new mother-in-law to hold on to her wedding ring until she was ready to wear it in front of her friends. The new married couple and Mother Crosson were bursting with excitement, but not a one mentioned the secret during the evening.

and afterward Mr. and Mrs. Joe Crosson climbed back into the open-cockpit Stearman biplane and flew home to Fairbanks.

Joe, Lillian, and Mother Crosson had been invited to dinner that evening with Clarence and Mary Burglin, a couple in Fairbanks. Joe and Lillian left the airport and went straight to the Burglins to join Mother Crosson, who was already there. At some point during the evening, Lillian took Mother Crosson aside in the bedroom and told her she and Joe were now married. She asked her new mother-in-law to hold on to her wedding ring until she was ready to wear it in front of her friends. The new married couple and Mother Crosson were bursting with excitement, but not a one mentioned the secret during the evening.

The next day Lillian was having lunch at the counter in the Model Cafe when local newspaper reporter Bob Bartlett plopped down on the seat next to her. He smiled coyly at her and asked, "Are you and Joe married? I hear you got married yesterday."

Lillian was startled. She felt that if word got out in the newspaper, they might as well kiss their honeymoon goodbye. She didn't answer, and her eyes pleaded with Bartlett not to publish the news. "I won't tell your secret," he said, pleased to be on the inside of such a good piece of Fairbanks information but respecting Joe and Lillian enough to help them out.

～

Several days later, as Joe and Lillian prepared to leave Fairbanks for their honeymoon, Joe's old friend Clark Bassett agreed to drive them and Mother Crosson to Chitina, where they would catch the train to Cordova and the steamship. Clark broke the news to Joe that the secret of the marriage was out, and that their friends were looking for them. The gang of pilots and other friends planned to block the road out of town, apprehend the couple, and have some fun with them.

"Move over," Joe ordered as he slid behind the steering wheel of Clark's car. At the edge of town Joe and his three passengers faced a makeshift blockade formed by their friends.

"Hold on, we're going through!" Joe yelled as he floored the accelerator. In the backseat, Lillian and Mother Crosson hid their eyes and only opened them after the men in the front seat shouted and laughed. Their friends had scattered, then rushed to their own vehicles and tried to follow the couple's getaway car. The pursuers soon gave up and returned to Fairbanks.

Joe, Lillian, and Joe's mother waited to board the train in Chitina, but when it arrived, they were embarrassed to see passengers with a large banner that offered wedding congratulations. Only slowly did they realize that the celebration was not for them, but for a couple from Cordova who were also embarking on a honeymoon.

In Seattle, Joe and Lillian officially announced their marriage, and the news traveled over the wires to the rest of the country. People around the United States cared about Joe because they had cheered him, Eielson, and Wilkins on in Antarctica, and they had mourned with him when his sister Marvel was killed. More recently he was known to them as the arctic pilot who led an international effort to find the fallen hero Ben Eielson.

Society pages proclaimed Joe a "domesticated eagle" and offered up headlines such as "Lindbergh of the Far North Takes Flight with Cupid" and "Arctic Hero Takes Bride on Aerial Honeymoon." Photos with the stories showed the happy couple sitting together or standing in the breeze next to a new airplane.

The newlyweds traveled for several weeks. Joe had promised Ole Eielson, Ben's father, he would visit him in Ben's hometown of Hatton, North Dakota. Joe and Lillian were treated like royalty by North Dakotans, who considered Ben a hero and greatly appreciated Joe's efforts to find him in Siberia. They toured the state and were received at the state capitol by the governor.

They also traveled to California, where Joe test-flew a new Ryan airplane with Lillian in the co-pilot's seat. It was her first experience with loops and other aerobatics. The young bride's stomach was not as tough as her husband's, and she remembers that they were "all over the sky" as Joe put the craft through its paces.

They made a trip to Pasadena Hospital, where Joe's sister Zelma

Society pages proclaimed Joe a "domesticated eagle" and offered up headlines such as "Lindbergh of the Far North Takes Flight with Cupid" and "Arctic Hero Takes Bride on Aerial Honeymoon."

Lillian remembers the years from 1930 to 1940 in Fairbanks as "a wonderful period of life, the best years we had together."

worked as a nurse. Although he was healthy at the time, Joe had suffered several attacks of appendicitis, and doctors had strongly encouraged him to have his appendix removed. Zelma made arrangements, and Joe grudgingly entered the hospital. As the operation approached, he had second thoughts and almost walked out. Only much talk and encouragement from his family and new bride convinced him to follow through with the surgery, from which he recovered rapidly.

$\sim$

AFTER THEIR HONEYMOON, Joe and Lillian returned to Fairbanks to settle down to married life. Lillian remembers the years from 1930 to 1940 in Fairbanks as "a wonderful period of life, the best years we had together." Married women of the day rarely worked outside the home, and Lillian gave up her job with the F.E. Company. However, she still starred in local theatrical productions and danced in community shows while Joe continued his career in aviation. Their social group included mostly people involved with aviation.

In December 1930, Lillian got a good lesson in the difficulties of being the wife of a bush pilot. Joe took her along on a trip to Nome, where he landed the Fairchild 71 on sea ice next to the town and taxied the ski plane close to the beach to secure it for the night. Joe and Lillian were welcomed to town by pilot Grant Elliot and his wife, Barbara, who invited the newlyweds into their home. Grant and Joe spent the next day and part of the evening going over business while Barbara and Lillian visited.

Sometime during that evening a man ran to the Elliot house and breathlessly announced that the sea ice near Nome was breaking up and moving. The Fairchild was in danger. Joe and Grant grabbed their coats and the five-gallon can of oil that was kept warm in the kitchen and rushed out. On the way to the beach, Joe told Grant, "If I can fly it off the ice, I'll head for Golovin." Lillian suddenly realized the urgency of the situation: the Fairchild was in danger of falling into the ocean or drifting out to sea.

By the time she reached the beach, the entire town had shown up to watch the spectacle. Lillian began to panic when she discovered that the local Coast Guard observer from Nome had rowed Joe to the wandering ice floe and just dropped him off. She ran to the Coast Guard observer and begged him to take her out to the plane as well.

"If he's going to die, then let me die, too!" she pleaded. Lillian remembered that the man was tall and stoic: he simply turned his back, ignored her sobs, and watched the drama on the ice floe.

Joe, in the meanwhile, was tending to business. He poured the oil in the motor, and without preheating the engine, managed to bring it to life. With barely enough room to maneuver, he was able to coax the Fairchild to flying speed and ease the plane into the air before it reached the end of the floating chunk of ice. Lillian sobbed as she watched his plane disappear.

Grant sent a message to Golovin, seventy-five miles away and the nearest place with good ice for a ski landing. The people there placed kerosene lanterns to mark out a runway on the sea ice, which was still holding fast to shore at that location. Lillian waited for an hour by the radiophone for word of Joe's fate. He finally called to tell her he was safe. But he couldn't return to Nome while the plane was on skis. No roads connected the towns, and the newlyweds were stranded in separate locations. It was two days before they were reunited.

Lillian had just endured her first frightening experience as a pilot's wife. She and the wives of other pilots became a close-knit bunch. More than anyone else, they understood and shared the worry each time their husbands flew off. Each of them experienced occasional nights walking the floor, praying for a safe return from a flight long overdue. The other wives were there to help until they could celebrate a joyous reunion, or mourn a tragic ending. The wives may have appeared standoffish to other townsfolk, but in times of need, the wives of the pilots had to band together for support.

The new Mrs. Crosson took on the role of hostess to visiting pilots, mechanics, and dignitaries in the world of aviation, and she excelled at it. She also devoted time to dog mushing. During the search for Ben Eielson in Siberia, a band of Chukchi Eskimos had given Joe a white

Lillian began to panic when she discovered that the local Coast Guard observer from Nome had rowed Joe to the wandering ice floe and just dropped him off.

▶ *Lillian plays with Nanuk in Fairbanks, where the furry white dog was the leader in her small sled-dog team.*

male puppy, which he brought home for Lillian. Nanuk grew up to be a longhaired, strong, and loyal friend, and Lillian wanted to raise an entire team just like him. Wherever he flew, Joe kept on the lookout for a longhaired, white, female sled dog to breed with Nanuk. He finally found just the right one in Nenana and borrowed her for a couple of months. The resulting pups formed Lillian's sled team, and she and Joe enjoyed driving the dogs on trips close to home. Lillian laughed as she remembered, "Everyone said Joe went to the dogs."

On July 16, 1931, Joseph E. Crosson Jr. was born. The sunny-natured pilot couldn't have been happier. The other pilots dropped by St. Joseph's Hospital to see the new baby. The first was Jimmy Mattern, a round-the-world flier who had just been rescued after crashing in Siberia and was staying in Fairbanks. Joe, the proud papa who never stopped teasing others, charged Jimmy a dollar to view his first son.

The dollar was a prized piece of Joe's "short snorter." Short snorters, a tradition with military pilots, consisted of a roll of dollar bills signed by other pilots and taped together end to end. Joe's snorter included dollar bills signed by Charles Lindbergh, Wiley Post, and other famous pilots.

Short snorters, a tradition with military pilots, consisted of a roll of dollar bills signed by other pilots and taped together end to end.

~

LIFE IN FAIRBANKS was ever-changing in the Crosson household. During the winter of 1931, Joe and Lillian lived in a house near the end of town at Tenth and Cushman Streets. As was relatively common then, they took in a high school girl as a boarder. She was Ruth Lawlor, the daughter of a gold mining family in the Circle Mining District, more than one hundred miles north of Fairbanks.

As in most outlying mining communities, no formal schooling was available in the Circle district. Primary reading, writing, and arithmetic were taught to children at home, but for high school instruction, the students had to go to Fairbanks. In exchange for baby-sitting and light housework, Ruth received room and board with the Crossons. They enjoyed her company and help, and she felt lucky to live with them because life in the Crosson household was easygoing and fun.

More than fifty years later, Ruth remembered how "Joe seemed to always be cheerful and nice to me." She slept upstairs in the small house, and her days would begin when "Joe would bang on the ceiling with a broomstick to wake me up to go to school."

Ruth also recalled a colorful incident when Fannie and Joe Quigley visited the house. The Quigleys had liked Joe since before the near-fateful flight to their Kantishna mine in 1927.

"Little Joe was in his chair," Ruth related, and Lillian was feeding him. "He kept turning away because he didn't want to eat it. 'Give me

With his instinctive sense of direction, he found their destination under conditions that today would require specialized navigation instruments.

that kid, I'll get him to eat,' she [Fannie Quigley] said, only she added a few words to it. Gee whiz, he was scared of her." Lillian would have no part in handing over Little Joe.

By the end of the school year, the Crossons had rented a smaller, two-bedroom house on Fifth Avenue, closer to the center of town. A few weeks later, Ruth headed back to her parents' home.

Joe enjoyed sharing his love of aviation with his family. During late 1931 he took Lillian and baby Joe in the open-cockpit Stearman on a flight from Fairbanks to the Park Strip, an early airport in Anchorage, to begin a vacation outside the Territory. It was winter, so he put blankets and a heavy sleeping bag on the floor of the Stearman so that Lillian and little Joe Jr. could curl up inside during the three-hour trip. But after several hours, Lillian sensed that the plane was circling. She peeked out of the sleeping bag into a snowstorm so thick she couldn't see the ground. She ducked back into the warmth to tend to the baby.

Frightening thoughts raced through her mind. Lillian trusted her husband's ability to bring them safely to earth, but after seeing the snowstorm, she wondered where they could land. An isolated, snow-covered lake in the middle of nowhere seemed the most likely.

The plane appeared to circle endlessly before she felt their descent and landing. But where? Lillian steeled herself for a difficult experience even as she knew that Joe had the skills to make sure they survived. The plane stopped and Joe opened the sleeping bag.

"Where are we?" Lillian asked.

Joe smiled and said, "We're at the strip in Anchorage." With his instinctive sense of direction, he found their destination under conditions that today would require specialized navigation instruments.

Joe and Lillian's second son, Don, was born July 23, 1934. The children filled the house with hubbub, toys, and fun. The small rented house on Fifth Avenue seemed to get smaller every day. So Joe and Lillian bought a large lot on the north side of the Chena River and had a house built for themselves.

The cheerful white house was of conventional peaked-roof design typical to the era and featured an automatic coal furnace. They situated the house so there was enough room on the lot for another

▲ Joe and Lillian with Lillian's dog team.

residence. Lillian dreamed of someday building a log home there, but in the meantime the space was used for a garden and playground, and eventually for a track for their boys' little race car.

Joe decided his young sons need a little car to drive, so he built one. Gathering an assortment of stray wheels, aircraft tubing, the nose cone from a Lockheed Electra, and a one-cylinder Maytag washing machine gas motor, he created the car in his basement shop. He also built the large oval track for the little racer.

Don could barely see over the steering wheel when Joe introduced him to the thrill of driving. But by the time Bob was born in 1938, young Joe Jr. and Don were already expert drivers—although Don recalls that at the age of four or five, he drove over his father's foot. The Crossons' race car was the talk of the neighborhood, and the sound of the motor was like the jingle of an ice cream truck. Kids showed up from all over to drive the little car.

▲ The Crosson family offers holiday greetings in a card from Fairbanks. From left, they are Joe, Joe Jr., Bob, Lillian, and Don.

Don and Myrtle Adler lived next door to Joe and Lillian, and their daughter Joanne remembers that driving the car was a special thrill. "We all had so much fun driving that car," she said. "I think everyone lost control and ran it off the track at least once, but we sure loved it."

Joe was a doting father who enjoyed his sons and played with them every day. On his return from a business trip to New York, Joe brought back four huge, stuffed panda bears, one for each son and one for neighbor Joanne Adler. The sons also got a railroad set that seems to have been as popular with the father and his friends as with the kids. Lillian remembers one Christmas when a couple of pilots stopped by the house to visit with Joe. Before long, "There they were in the living room on the floor playing with the boys' new model railroad train set, with the boys just watching."

Joe continued to be a well-respected member of the community. During late 1935, he was drafted by the Fourth Division Democratic Club as its candidate for senator in the Territorial Legislature. Joe was flattered by the offer but announced he would not run, citing his duties with his employer and his devotion to airline expansion in Alaska. Lillian later recalled that his employer at that time, Pan American, "didn't want Joe involved in politics." To the great disappointment of the local Democratic party, who saw him as an unbeatable candidate, Joe Crosson was never on the ballot.

In 1936, Joe and Don Adler chaired the Fairbanks Ice Carnival, a winter event celebrated by the entire community. Don's wife, Myrtle, pitched in to help, and Lillian coordinated the entertainment for the successful event.

Although very busy with work, Joe loved the time he spent with his wife and children. He maintained a workshop in the basement so the boys could learn about machines and tools. He delighted in bestowing nicknames on each member, laughing with "Lilli Kapilli," "Jody Pody," "Donnie Ponnie," and "Bobbie Dee." A number of events involving Joe during the 1930s carved his name ever deeper into aviation history, but family life came first.

To the great disappointment of the local Democratic party, who saw him as an unbeatable candidate, Joe Crosson was never on the ballot.

Alaska Airways manager Arthur Johnson and Joe

12

MERCY PILOT

Barrow, Alaska, March 1931. Joe Crosson was bundled in a heavy fur parka and pants, moosehide mittens, and fur boots, but still he shivered in the open-cockpit Stearman biplane as he flew in minus-30-degree temperatures. Little had changed since his first flight to Barrow in 1927. On the positive side, the Stearman's air-cooled motor was far more dependable than the liquid-cooled motors of earlier planes, and Crosson had a great deal more experience than he had in 1927. However, the plane did not carry a radio. No weather forecasts were available. No runways existed north of the Brooks Range. No one could help him if things went wrong.

Crosson knew the risks, but more lives were at stake than his own. An epidemic was threatening Barrow, and his cargo was diphtheria serum.

Howling winds scudded snow across the rough sea ice as Crosson reached the tiny frozen community of Barrow, searching for a spot to land. In this farthest north part of the Territory of Alaska, the sun had been gone for most of the winter and had only ventured above the horizon for the past few days. He found a short strip the villagers had quickly marked out on the sea ice, throttled back, and brought the Stearman down.

April 2, 1931
Amelia Earhart reaches 18,415 feet in a Pitcairn Autogiro, setting the woman's altitude record for rotor-wing aircraft (a relative of the helicopter).

◄ *Arthur Johnson hands Joe Crosson a carton with diphtheria serum for his first flight to Barrow with the lifesaving medicine. Joe delivered the serum to the remote northern village March 7, 1931, in the open-cockpit Stearman.*

People were excited as Crosson handed over the lifesaving packages of serum.

It was still very unusual for a plane to land in Barrow during the winter. Very few planes crossed the Brooks Range. Dr. Henry Greist and all of the able-bodied people in the village met the plane as it bumped to a stop on the makeshift runway. People were excited as Crosson handed over the lifesaving packages of serum. He also handed out the magazines, tobacco, and fruit that Alaskan Airways staff had loaded into the plane for the villagers.

Greist told Crosson that during Sunday services several days earlier, when more than two hundred Barrow parishioners were gathered in the church, some were coughing and feverish. He later diagnosed one full-blown case of diphtheria and he feared that other parishioners were in danger of contracting the deadly, highly contagious disease.

Greist had immediately telegraphed the Territorial Health Commission, followed by a wire to Governor George Parks in Juneau. He explained that the limited supply of serum in Barrow was old and inadequate for immediate needs. All residents of the village were in imminent danger, and new diphtheria antitoxin was desperately needed.

The next day, March 5, 1931, Governor Parks wired a Fox Film crew in Seward and asked if they would carry the antitoxin on their scheduled March 12 flight with Alaskan Airways to Barrow, where they planned to do some filming. The crew agreed, but the Barrow situation was deteriorating as more people became ill. Parks contacted Alaskan Airways directly in Fairbanks, and Joe Crosson stepped forward to pilot the plane with the precious cargo.

In Barrow, Crosson secured the plane, then accepted Greist's invitation to spend the night. He didn't get much rest because the Greists kept him up very late talking. He learned that the epidemic first started in Point Hope around Christmas. From there it worked its way north to Wainwright, where two people died from the disease before diphtheria was eventually diagnosed at Barrow.

Months had passed since the Greists had talked with someone from as far away as Fairbanks. They were thirsty for news from the south, so Joe filled them in for hours. The *Fairbanks Daily News-Miner*

▶ *Pilot Robbie Robbins (left), manager Arthur Johnson, and Joe talk over the flight before the second diphtheria serum flights to Barrow.*

said of Crosson: "He talked so much that he finally got a sore throat and thought he had the diphtheria himself."

Crosson decided not to challenge the Brooks Range again on his return flight. He left Barrow on Sunday morning, March 8, and followed the route he had pioneered four years earlier. He pointed the Stearman southwest along the coast toward Kotzebue and landed at Wainwright to check on gas supplies for the upcoming Fox Film flight. As he continued along the coast, he ran into snow and fog that forced

He had covered about two thousand miles over the most forbidding part of Alaska in winter, a feat that would have taken dog teams weeks to accomplish.

him to spend the night at Point Lay, a tiny coastal Eskimo village. Weather improved, and the next morning he flew all the way to the Interior Indian village of Ruby on the Yukon River.

Crosson arrived back in Fairbanks on March 10, three days after leaving for Barrow. He had covered about two thousand miles over the most forbidding part of Alaska in winter, a feat that would have taken dog teams weeks to accomplish.

Greist telegraphed of further outbreaks of diphtheria in Barrow and Wainwright. On March 12, Crosson and fellow Alaskan Airways pilot Robbie Robbins headed west and north along the coast with the Fox Film crew and a second shipment of antitoxin. The passengers were spared the frigid temperatures Joe had endured on his flight the week before. This flight was made in the relative comfort of two of the company's Fairchild 71 cabin monoplanes.

Crosson and Robbins flew from Fairbanks to Kotzebue, intending to follow the coast northeast to Barrow. Driving blizzards and foul weather born in Siberia and the arctic ice pack strike the coast with no warning. After refueling at Kotzebue the pilots pushed on but the weather turned bad. Bouncing roughly in the wind and blowing snow, Robbins turned back to Kotzebue with his passengers. Crosson saw Robbins' Fairchild bank and disappear behind him. He thought about turning around as well, then looked at the package of serum. He pressed on past Point Hope and again spent the night with the Eskimos at Point Lay.

The storm blew through the night and was still in full force in the morning, but Crosson took off anyway. The Fairchild was tossed around as Crosson battled headwinds and buffeting to make it to his fuel cache at Wainwright. He was worried. He'd used more gas fighting the storms than planned, so he didn't have enough aviation gas in Wainwright to complete the trip. The only other fuel in the village was common gasoline, used by the Eskimos for their outboard motors. Ordinary gasoline, with a lower octane rating than av gas, provides less power and fouls spark plugs in airplane engines, sometimes causing them to fail. But Crosson had no choice. He topped his tanks with gasoline and pressed on.

Crosson won the gamble and landed with the second shipment of serum at Barrow with the fuel gauge on empty. It was Friday the 13th, a lucky day in Barrow. The diphtheria serum was safe in hand. Dr. Greist treated the villagers and no lives were lost, due in part to the swift delivery.

The winter flights to Barrow in 1931 were two of many during his career that defined Crosson as a pilot with few equals. Although the delivery of serum was considered a monumental accomplishment to those in Barrow, it was closer to a day's work for one of Alaska's most experienced pilots. He was now twenty-eight years old.

Although the delivery of serum was considered a monumental accomplishment to those in Barrow, it was closer to a day's work for one of Alaska's most experienced pilots.

Wiley Post and Joe with a string of ptarmigan

13

JOE'S FRIEND WILEY

Fairbanks, June 1931. Wiley Post powered up the big radial engine and pointed the *Winnie Mae* down the remote Alaska beach, ready for takeoff. He and navigator Harold Gatty were nearly a week into an attempt to set a new speed record for an around-the-world flight. They had only to traverse Alaska and Canada to arrive in New York and the record would be theirs.

The trip had gone flawlessly until the day before in Siberia. The *Winnie Mae* had become stuck on a muddy runway and Post lost half a day trying to communicate to the Russians to get a team of horses to pull the plane free. Since then the two-man crew had picked their way across Siberia in miserable weather. Post flew the white Lockheed Vega many extra miles finding a way around, over, or through storms.

Adding to the harrowing experience were the inaccurate Russian maps. If navigator Gatty had relied on the maps, Post would have flown into a mountain. Instead they were forced to climb above the clouds so Gatty could take a bearing from the sun. The extra miles took a toll on fuel. The Vega's gas gauge was dancing on empty when they spotted the clear strip of beach at Solomon, Alaska.

Back on American soil they hoped that things would be looking up. They obtained av gas at the Solomon trading post and their next

May 25-28, 1931
W. E. Lees and F. A. Brossi set a world endurance record without refueling, flying a Bellanca Packard diesel airplane for 85 hours, 32 minutes.

◄ *Joe Crosson holds a string of ptarmigan game birds that he and Wiley Post bagged on a hunting trip through Alaska in 1934, while Wiley looks on. Wiley was planning to move to Alaska and join Joe in a gold mining operation.*

145

▶ Wiley Post shows the trophy brown bear that he shot in a hunt on the Copper River flats.

stop was Fairbanks—only a few more hours before they could relax with Wiley Post's good friend Joe Crosson, take a bath, and sleep.

Post started the takeoff run down the beach. Nearing takeoff speed the Vega suddenly slowed and mired in the muddy beach sand. Post cut power to the Wasp radial, but it was too late. In slow motion the plane went up on its nose, bending both propeller tips. With rocks, a hammer, and a few hand tools, the flyers straightened the prop tips as best they could and tried the takeoff again. This time Post got the Vega into the air and nursed the craft to Fairbanks, where Joe Crosson waited.

Joe and Wiley first met during 1929 while Joe was ferrying planes between various states and Wiley was taking miscellaneous flying jobs. At one point, Wiley needed a ride from Oklahoma to California. Joe was heading that way and had an empty seat.

Joe and Wiley instantly hit it off. Both pilots enjoyed wide-open spaces, found pleasure in hunting and fishing, and had strong ambitions. They loved flying and everything about it, from the challenge of building and repairing planes to the thrill of soaring through the air. That was enough to cement a long and lasting friendship.

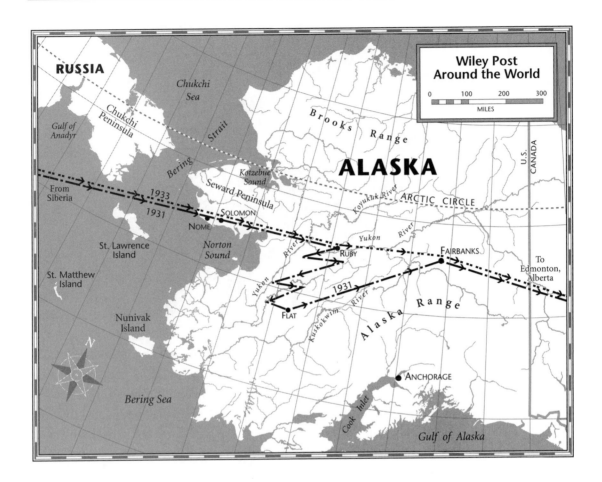

In California, Joe took Wiley to meet his parents in San Diego. Elizabeth and Esler frequently opened their home to wayward (often broke) airmen needing a warm meal and a clean bed. The short, stocky pilot from Oklahoma was immediately part of the family.

Wiley Post was an anomaly among commercial aviators. Pilots' very lives depend on visual acuity and depth perception, yet Wiley had only one eye. He had lost the other in an oil field accident years earlier in his home state of Oklahoma. But Wiley had proved his flying ability, and the Civil Aeronautics Authority issued him a special waiver to fly. Nevertheless, he still found it difficult to compete for flying jobs. Wiley began to dream of ways to make a name for himself in aviation, and the around-the-world trip plan was hatched.

▲ *Miners in Flat, Alaska, work to right Wiley Post's Winnie Mae. After flying lost over Interior Alaska for several hours on July 20, 1933, Post spotted the short airstrip at Flat, set up a landing, and ran off the end of the runway. Joe Crosson brought mechanics and parts from Fairbanks to repair the Winnie Mae.*

Once in Fairbanks, the mishap in Solomon behind them, Post and Gatty were in the capable hands of Joe Crosson, chief pilot for Alaskan Airways. Crosson had the *Winnie Mae* wheeled into the company hangar. The flyers were lucky: Alaskan Airways had a propeller on hand that fit the Wasp. While Post and Gatty grabbed three hours of sleep, Crosson had his mechanics go to work on the *Winnie Mae*. The mechanics were amazed at how well Post and Gatty had been able to straighten the prop with almost no tools, but they replaced the propeller and checked out the craft for other damage.

Crosson had a knack for being in the middle of historic aviation events. He didn't aspire to set records or make long marathon flights himself, focusing instead on his family and establishing aviation in the Territory of Alaska. Because of its location, Fairbanks was on the route of many record-setting flights. And when other pilots pursuing records needed help in Fairbanks, they needed Joe Crosson.

Repairs completed, the *Winnie Mae* lifted off from Fairbanks and finished the flight to New York. Post and Gatty made it around the world in less than nine days—a new record. A ticker tape parade greeted the aviators in New York City.

~

AFTER HIS RECORD-BREAKING flight with Harold Gatty, Wiley Post wanted more. He wanted to fly around the world again, only this time by himself. In July 1933 he took off alone in the *Winnie Mae* to follow the same route around the world as before. The flight went well through his refueling stop in Siberia. Wiley Post was well on the way to becoming the first person to fly alone around the world—and to breaking his own speed record as well.

From Siberia, clouds thickened and Wiley was forced to climb on top of the overcast. Mountains breaking through the clouds told him he was over Alaska. He found a break in the overcast next to the mountains and flew under the clouds. His recently installed automatic direction finder detected signals from radio antennas at major airfields. The direction finder allowed Wiley to home in on Nome,

▼ Fairbanks residents bid farewell and good luck to Wiley Post as he heads for Edmonton, Alberta, during his solo round-the-world flight in July 1933.

After seven hours of wandering in the sky he spotted a small runway at the town of Flat. Later Wiley recalled, "I was completely lost.

where he circled the radio antenna and headed toward Fairbanks. Wiley expected the direction finder to intercept the signal from Fairbanks en route so he could simply follow it to that city. But the instrument chose this time to malfunction.

Wiley got lost. For several hours all he could do was fly along half asleep, searching for landmarks or a place to land. He crossed and recrossed dozens of rivers, hills, and forests, never seeing anything that looked familiar. After seven hours of wandering in the sky he spotted a small runway at the town of Flat. Later Wiley recalled, "I was completely lost. I therefore headed back to Nome, and on my way I spied what I later found was Flat."

Wiley's arrival on July 20 startled the gold miners in the tiny Interior community. The dusty 700-foot-long landing strip was far too short for Wiley's fast craft and he overshot the runway, coming to rest in a ditch with the *Winnie Mae* perched precariously on her nose. The propeller was badly bent and the right landing gear was torn almost completely from the plane. His chances of completing his record-breaking flight seemed dashed.

In one respect Flat was a good place for Wiley to come down. The mining town had radio communications and word of his mishap was quickly relayed to Joe Crosson. Joe, who was now chief pilot for Pacific Alaska Airways, and mechanics Loren Fernald and Larry Davis climbed into a Fairchild 71, carrying a new propeller and enough tools and parts to patch the *Winnie Mae* back together.

By the time Joe touched down in Flat, the miners of that community had erected a tripod from spruce poles and had righted the *Winnie Mae*. Joe and Wiley surveyed the damage before Joe sent his friend to get some sleep, rolled up his sleeves, and joined in the repairs. By dawn Joe and the mechanics had patched the landing gear back together and replaced the propeller. Wiley again headed for Fairbanks, this time following Joe.

Wiley climbed out of his craft in front of the Pacific Alaska hangar. Leaving mechanic Jim Hutchison to work his magic on the landing gear and radioman Bob Gleason to fix the direction finder, Joe and Wiley headed to the Crosson home. Joe and Lillian had been married for three years. Their first son, Joe Jr., was an active two-year-old, and Lillian was expecting their second child. Joe and Lillian were a happy couple who opened their home to friends old and new.

"I thought Wiley should go right to bed and sleep when he and Joe came in," Lillian recalls. "But he and Joe stayed in the living room most of the time talking aviation, it was in their blood. Finally, he did get a couple of hours when they were fixing the plane.

"When he got up I insisted that he should eat something before leaving but he didn't want to. Finally he agreed to have a bite and asked for plain mush. He always claimed that the mush made him sleepy and he almost fell asleep several times after he left Fairbanks."

Wiley managed to stay awake for the trip to Edmonton, Alberta. And when he landed in New York, he became the first person to complete a solo flight around the world. But the Alaska bug had taken hold of him. Within months Wiley traveled back to Alaska to spend time with Joe Crosson.

"Wiley loved Alaska and Joe's help made it even better for him," Lillian said. "Whenever they were together they talked flying, hunting, or gold mining. Wiley stayed at the house and the two of them were constantly on the go."

With Joe at the controls of a Stearman biplane, the men took off to the Copper River flats to hunt brown bear along the southern coast of the Territory. Days were spent hunting. Evenings, around the smoky campfire, they told flying stories. After a couple of days hunting, Wiley shot a large bear. After that trip Joe took his friend ptarmigan hunting in the Interior and on assorted fishing trips. With such a competent and fun-loving guide as Joe, Wiley was finding Alaska more like home all the time.

Lillian remembered that Post was taken by the northern territory.

"Wiley loved everything about Alaska and he was very interested in mining. At the time we were partners in two mining operations, the Hi-Yu and the Mastodon Mining Company. Wiley wanted to know every detail about the operation and he and Joe talked about going into a mining operation together."

Wiley would be back.

Wiley managed to stay awake for the trip to Edmonton, Alberta. And when he landed in New York, he became the first person to complete a solo flight around the world.

Mt. McKinley "20360 ft." Alaska.

Commercial photographer Charles Camm

14

JOE AND THE MOUNTAIN

Mount McKinley, July 1930. Few modern travelers to Mount McKinley know about the pilot who pioneered flightseeing to and around the mountain, confirmed the altitude of the lofty peak, and was the first to land an airplane on its slopes. That pilot was Joe Crosson.

Early pilots in Alaska were dependent on a simple compass, dead reckoning, their memories, and natural landmarks to navigate from place to place. On clear days, Mount McKinley—also known as Denali (the Great One)—stands like a lighthouse high above the countryside. Viewed from Anchorage, it rises in the northwest; to a pilot flying south from Fairbanks, it stands in the southwest; and when traveling by air southward from Nome, it peeks above the southeast horizon. Stark and white in summer sun, soft pink in the half light of early spring and late fall, or faintly glowing in the moon's light during midwinter, the mountain is a beacon made of solid rock coated in ice and snow.

It was a beautiful July evening in 1930 when Crosson greeted some special passengers. Alaska Governor George Parks led a party that included Territorial officials, the general manager of McKinley Tourist & Transportation Company, and Crosson's own boss Arthur W.

July 21, 1930

Marine Corps pilot Capt. A. H. Page, accompanied by a safety pilot, flies 1,000 miles under a sealed cockpit hood, relying only on instruments to maintain control.

◄ *Charles Cann stands in front of the Alaskan Airways' Super Swallow on a perfect day to view Mount McKinley. Joe Crosson pioneered flights in and around Mount McKinley National Park.*

▲ *Joe Crosson (right) poses next to Alaska Governor George Parks, accompanied by several officials, before a flight through Mount McKinley National Park in July 1930. The governor called it "the best trip I have ever taken in an airplane."*

Johnson. The dependable Fairchild 71 with a Wasp radial engine was chosen for the flight to Mount McKinley.

From the earliest Alaska flights in the mid-1920s, passengers had enjoyed spectacular views of the mountain from the air. But this was the first attempt to cater to tourist interests using flying as a dependable way to visit North America's tallest peak, and the first time a park concessionaire offered aerial tours.

Crosson entertained the party in the blue Alaskan sky for more than three hours, treating them to a constantly changing panorama of glaciers, lakes, mountains, rivers, and wildlife. He flew across Muldrow Glacier at 9,000 feet and straight at the huge mountain, then to Wonder Lake and eventually back to the Savage River Camp in the soft light of the midsummer evening.

The governor was enthusiastic about the flight:

It was the best trip I have ever taken in an airplane. I have never seen anything like it. We were flying at an elevation of 9,000 feet and from that elevation it was possible to see Mount Foraker as well as Mount McKinley. We headed for the northeast ridge, the one used by mountain climbing expeditions. It almost looked like you could touch it from where we were.

The whole thing was stupendous. The glaciers and knife-like ridges were revealed in great detail. When we turned to come back we flew straight down the glacier. The huge pits in the moraines and crevasses in the ice were clearly visible. Altogether, it was the prettiest thing I have ever seen.

After the plane returned to Fairbanks, the device would be recalibrated, and it could be determined whether the mountain was closer to 20,000 or to 25,000 feet tall.

Governor Parks saw more of Mount McKinley National Park on the flight than on all his numerous previous ground trips to the region. The party estimated they saw two thousand sheep and the same number of caribou. Flightseeing in the park became a popular activity for visitors to the Territory.

~

CROSSON'S NEXT MCKINLEY flight helped determine the mountain's elevation above sea level. While it was widely accepted that McKinley was about 20,300 feet tall, no accurate measurements had been made. A number of Alaskans argued that the mountain rose closer to 25,000 feet. Pilot Matt Niemenen had flown over the peak in 1930, but his plane was not equipped with instruments accurate enough to provide a definitive elevation.

Crosson took off in his workhorse Fairchild 71 from Weeks Field in Fairbanks just before one o'clock in the afternoon of August 29, 1931. The 425-horsepower Wasp radial engine had been freshly rebuilt for the flight. The plane was carrying four different altimeters. One of the instruments, strapped to a wing strut, was a Weather Bureau metrograph, a device that recorded altitude, temperature, and humidity. After the plane returned to Fairbanks, the device would be recalibrated, and it could be determined whether the mountain was closer to 20,000 or to 25,000 feet tall.

The flight was quite a production. The event was being recorded on film for release on newsreels throughout the nation, which was a

"We hit a down current and dropped about 600 or 700 feet on the leeward side of the mountain. Circling about to the other side or the windward side, an up current carried us up about 700 feet in about 10 minutes, with hardly an exertion on the part of the plane."

promotional coup for Alaskan Airways. A sound engineer for Fox Movietone News and Hearst Metrotone News was aboard the plane with Crosson. Another Fairchild 71, piloted by Ed Young, carried a cameraman. Crosson and Young had worked out a series of hand signals so they could communicate for maneuvering their planes into positions that would help the cameraman get the best shots.

They left shortly after noon on August 29 with about one hundred gallons of gasoline in each plane. Although the morning weather report for the park showed that the mountain was visible, scattered clouds looked rather thick toward the mountain, and there was no guarantee the top would be clear.

Crosson climbed slowly and at about 12,500 feet he could see the summit. By this time the planes were fairly close to the mountain. Crosson's plane climbed faster than Young's and flew over the top several times while the photographer in Young's plane recorded the event on film. Pilots and passengers got a good view of both the north and south peaks and, on one pass, dropped a box with a piece of leather inscribed with the names of the pilots and passengers and the date to document the flight.

At one point Crosson's plane encountered a friendly updraft and climbed rapidly, crossing the summit with ease. Within minutes, he learned more about the peculiarities of air movement around the mountain. In his log, Crosson wrote that "we hit a down current and dropped about 600 or 700 feet on the leeward side of the mountain. Circling about to the other side or the windward side, an up current carried us up about 700 feet in about 10 minutes, with hardly an exertion on the part of the plane. Getting a few hundred feet away from the mountain these upward and downward currents were not noticeable. It was when we were within about 100 feet of the mountain that they were effective."

During the flight, Crosson took the opportunity to analyze his plane's performance and learn more about its capabilities. His log recorded that the plane "performed perfectly every minute of the way; if a turn was made rather sharply a little altitude was lost, but that was of little account. The motor too functioned at its best. It was

impossible to get the carburetor adjusted permanently for altitude at above 17,000 feet, and about every ten minutes it took some time to get the right spot on the carburetor."

The summit flight completed, the planes headed for Savage River and descended with a sense of urgency. "We realized that it was necessary to get below the clouds which were closing in on us," Crosson recorded, "and also to renew our gasoline supply which was getting low, at the Savage River Camp." After landing and refueling at Savage River, both planes returned to Fairbanks, arriving a little less than six hours after leaving Weeks Field.

Movie fans were thrilled to get a bird's-eye view of the huge mountain as the film was later shown in theaters across the nation. The mountain's mysteries were being explained one by one. It wasn't possible to get exact elevation measurements, but Crosson's observations and the results from the scientific instruments showed that the summit was slightly above 20,000 feet, and nowhere near 25,000 feet.

▲ *A group of tourists enjoyed an early flightseeing trip through Mount McKinley National Park in the comfort of a Fairchild 71 monoplane, piloted by Joe (far left).*

Stearman C28 on Muldrow Glacier

15

ON MAJESTIC SLOPES

Mount McKinley, spring 1932. With spring racing toward summer, Mount McKinley was the focus of two expeditions, the first major activity on the mountain in several years. Harry Liek, superintendent of Mount McKinley National Park, and Albert Lindley headed an expedition intent on becoming only the second party to ever reach the summit. Mountaineer and scientist Allen Carpé also led a climbing party, with the goal of using the mountain's elevation as a platform for a study of cosmic rays.

Lindley had studied the mountain and chosen a route to the summit while flying with Joe Crosson the previous summer. Now he hired Crosson to periodically fly over his team to check on their progress. By mid-April 1932, Lindley and his group were climbing the mountain. The expedition relied on the tried-and-true method of dogsled travel to get to the slopes. It took more than a week for three dog teams and the climbers to move their provisions 105 miles from park headquarters to base camp on Muldrow Glacier.

Allen Carpé, also hoping to establish camp on the Muldrow, proposed something new for his expedition. Over dinner at the Crosson home, Carpé explained that he wanted to move his team and their supplies as close to the mountain as possible by airplane. He

April 19, 1932

Robert Goddard successfully flies a gyroscopically controlled liquid-fuel rocket near Roswell, New Mexico.

◄ *Joe had taken off in the Fairchild 71 to drop supplies at the climbers' upper camp higher on the Muldrow Glacier while the Stearman C2B piloted by Jerry Jones awaited on the glacier.*

▲ *Jerry Jones in a Stearman C2B starts his turn into Mount McKinley's Muldrow Glacier on May 3, 1932, on a flight to support mountain climbers.*

wanted the airplane to actually land them on McKinley's Muldrow Glacier. No plane had ever landed on the mountain, but Crosson thought the plan would work.

On the morning of April 25, 1932, Carpé and team members Edward P. Beckwith and Theodore Koven were at the grocery store in Nenana, carefully weighing food and gear. Crosson was coming to Nenana to take them to the mountain. As the prearranged meeting time came and went, Carpé called the Alaskan Airways manager, Arthur Johnson. Johnson said Crosson had been delayed after damaging an airplane ski in the soft snow at Weeks Field in Fairbanks, but that he was now on his way. Johnson was skeptical that a plane could land on Muldrow Glacier, but he agreed to leave the decision to Crosson.

A short time later, Crosson landed the red-and-white, ski-equipped Fairchild 71 on the Tanana River ice at Nenana. Gear was carefully loaded into the plane as the climbers sized up the pilot they would entrust with their lives. Beckwith was immediately impressed with Joe's easygoing nature, noting that "Crosson seemed unconcerned about the prospect of attempting to land on the untried slopes of McKinley." Before noon the three men had piled in and Crosson eased the Fairchild into the air and headed toward Mount McKinley to see if he could find a favorable landing spot on the glacier.

The slopes of McKinley presented peculiar challenges to pilots. There were no trees or structures on the glacier to provide an indication of distance or scale. Boulders that were visible could have been five feet high or fifty as far as Crosson could tell. Winds tumbling over the crags and ledges of the mountain were worrisome, and a storm was on its way.

Crosson studied the surface and consulted with Carpé, who had a great deal of mountaineering experience. Once his decision was made, Crosson set up the landing. Tension filled the cabin as the plane flew toward the mountain and the climbers watched it grow larger and larger. Crosson guided the Fairchild in for a perfect landing at an elevation of about 5,600 feet. After the plane slid to a stop, Carpé enthusiastically shook the pilot's hand. Beckwith noted that Crosson took the landing "much as a matter of course, and lit a cigar before leaving the plane."

Following the historic landing, supplies were quickly unloaded so Crosson could take off before the building storm turned into a blizzard. Winds were increasing and visibility was decreasing. Joe instructed the climbers in hand-cranking the inertial starter on the engine cowling so that he could stay inside at the controls. He turned the Fairchild into the wind and gave the engine full throttle up the glacier.

The mountaineers stared after the plane as it disappeared into the swirling snow. They heard the motor noise stop far up the glacier, and they were concerned when Crosson didn't fly over their camp after takeoff. Carpé and Koven feared he had crashed, but a search on skis

Beckwith was immediately impressed with Joe's easygoing nature, noting that "Crosson seemed unconcerned about the prospect of attempting to land on the untried slopes of McKinley."

Crosson knew that a huge ridge was looming ahead, unseen in the driving snowstorm. He aborted the takeoff, fighting updrafts and gale-force winds to keep the plane on the glacier's surface.

turned up nothing. In fact, Crosson had just taken one of the most harrowing rides of his life—and he was still on the glacier.

The uphill takeoff run had lasted much longer than Crosson expected. He was finally able to fly the plane off the rough ice and climb to three hundred feet, but a sudden downdraft forced it back onto the glacier. The plane was still moving forward, up the glacier. Crosson knew that a huge ridge was looming ahead, unseen in the driving snowstorm. He aborted the takeoff, fighting updrafts and gale-force winds to keep the plane on the glacier's surface.

When he finally cut power to the engine, he was three miles up the glacier from the climbers' camp. Crosson considered his options. He could probably abandon the plane and get to the camp safely, but the wind would destroy the Fairchild, and everyone would be stranded. He had to secure the large plane against the wind.

The big wings on the Fairchild 71 were designed to fold up against the fuselage, allowing the plane to be stored in a relatively small space. Folding the wings now would give the Fairchild its best chance to survive the storm in one piece. But each wing was more than twenty feet long and three feet wide and weighed well over two hundred pounds. It took two strong men to fold them safely on a sunny summer afternoon. Crosson was alone on a mountain in a driving storm. The blowing snow stung his face and chilled his body as he fought to free and rotate the cumbersome wings.

Far below on the glacier, the three mountaineers also fought the storm. Hours later, with minds still focused on securing their equipment and surviving the storm, they were shocked to see Crosson emerge from the fog and walk into camp. Beckwith again found Joe to be "the same as usual—calm and matter-of-course." Relatively sheltered in their canvas tents that evening, the expedition members decided that Beckwith should return to Nenana with Crosson the following morning to obtain additional equipment, including a tent pole to replace one that snapped in the storm.

Early in the morning Crosson and the other men headed for the Fairchild, which was now visible as a small red spot far up the glacier. Crosson covered the engine with canvas and fired up the warming

stove. The men helped him unfold the wings and lock them back into
flying position. The plane's skis had frozen to the glacier, so they
rocked the wings by hand to break the skis loose. Finally, Joe was able
to start the engine. Beckwith climbed in, and this time Crosson
pointed the Fairchild down the glacier toward camp.

This takeoff run offered new challenges. Wind had carved the
snow into frozen parallel ridges on the glacier's surface, and Joe had to
cross the ridges at a ninety-degree angle until he reached flying speed.
The plane shuddered at each collision of the skis with the hard-packed
ridges. Beckwith described the harrowing takeoff as a "tough, long
ride," and he feared one of the skis would break off. The hammering
ceased as Joe eased the plane into the air. In a few seconds their
perilous takeoff run gave way to a glorious view of Mount McKinley
as the Fairchild climbed to safety.

▲ *Climbers (from left)*
Percy Olton Jr., Nicholas
Spadavecchia, and
Edward Beckwith check
climbing gear as pilot Joe
Crosson looks on. The
trusty Fairchild 71 sits
idling and ready to go
back to work.

▲ *Jerry Jones (left) and Joe Crosson stand on the Muldrow Glacier by the Stearman C2B piloted by Jones. Crosson's Fairchild 71 is in the background.*

Later that morning, over breakfast in Nenana, Crosson treated Beckwith to a classic understatement: "I have not often had a job like that to handle."

~

A week later, on May 3, Crosson and fellow Alaskan Airways pilot Walter J. (Jerry) Jones were ready to fly to McKinley with Beckwith and other scientists who were part of the Carpé group. They left from Birch Lake, east of Fairbanks: Jones piloting a Stearman and Crosson flying a

Fairchild 71, both equipped with skis. Beckwith climbed in with Jones to take pictures during the flight to the camp on the glacier. Crosson was joined by expedition members Nicholas Spadavecchia and Percy Olton Jr.

This time, the landings on the glacier were uneventful. At the glacier camp, they found a note from Carpé indicating that he and Koven had gone on to the head of the glacier to establish a camp at 11,000 feet. Crosson and Beckwith loaded several packages of supplies into the Fairchild for an airdrop at Carpé's new camp, and they took off with no problem.

The first order of business was to look for members of the Liek-Lindley expedition to see how they were doing. Crosson found them 17,000 feet and noted that the team had been able to cut a long series of steps into the ice. Next came the airdrop to Carpé. Although Beckwith had to struggle to keep the plane's door open in the slipstream, he managed to drop the packages. Later that day, pilots Crosson and Jones flew from the original glacier camp back to Fairbanks.

With no radios for communicating from the mountain, members of the Liek-Lindley expedition had hoped to complete their climb and be back at national park headquarters by May 15. From there they could telephone news about the climb to Fairbanks. Their predicted timetable was remarkably close: the phone message came through on Sunday, May 16. The climbers brought news of both triumph and tragedy, and immediately set in motion plans for another flight to Mount McKinley.

The expedition had indeed been successful and made history by climbing both the north and south summits of McKinley. But the triumph was overshadowed by the tragic news of the Carpé expedition.

Allen Carpé and Theodore Koven, Joe's passengers on the first flight to the mountain, were dead. They had skied into a crevasse as they were heading down to the lower glacier camp to rejoin the rest of their party, probably on May 9.

Carpé's body, trapped deep inside the glacier, was never recovered. Koven had been able to climb out of the crevasse but apparently died of his injuries and hypothermia before the Liek-Lindley climbers

The climbers brought news of both triumph and tragedy, and immediately set in motion plans for another flight to Mount McKinley.

▶ Jerry Jones adds gas to the Stearman from a five-gallon can through a funnel.

found him. Because of the treacherous crevasses, they left Koven's body on the glacier, wrapped in a tent, and marked the spot with a sled standing on end.

There was more bad news concerning the Carpé expedition. Beckwith was critically ill at the lower glacier camp. Nicholas Spadavecchia had left the camp several days earlier in an attempt to hike out for help. He was traveling in unfamiliar territory with limited provisions. He had not reached the ranger station and his whereabouts were unknown.

When the news reached Fairbanks on May 16, Crosson was in Barrow, and the rescue flight was assigned to Jerry Jones. Pioneering a new technique, Jones waited for the Fairbanks Fire Department to hose down the dirt runway and he successfully took off from the mud on skis. He flew in the open-cockpit Stearman to the lower glacier camp, where he helped Percy Olton bundle up the sick Beckwith and get him into the plane. Less than five hours after departing Fairbanks, Jones safely slid the Stearman to a stop on the Weeks Field mud. Beckwith soon recovered at the hospital.

Now only one climber, Percy Olton, was still on the mountain. On May 19, the fire department again hosed down the dirt strip at Weeks Field. This time Robbie Robbins—like Jones, a San Diego pilot recruited to Alaska by Crosson—lifted the Stearman off the mud and flew to the mountain to pick up Olton and to search for the missing Nicholas Spadavecchia. Weather on the mountain was poor. Although

◄ Jerry Jones lifts off of Weeks Field in Fairbanks, bound for Muldrow Glacier to rescue an ill climber, Edward Beckwith. The dirt runway was watered down by the Fairbanks Fire Department to allow Jones to take off on skis for a landing on the glacier.

Robbins managed a safe landing at the glacier camp, the Stearman's axle broke as he taxied in the soft snow. But as it turned out, Robbins was successful in finding Spadavecchia; the missing man had returned to the camp.

The next day, Jerry Jones flew from Fairbanks to Mount McKinley in a Fairchild 71 to search for Robbins. Flying above the glacier camp, Jones dropped a can of liquid lampblack and a paint brush to Robbins, who wrote in the snow: "S & O Safe Axle Broke."

Jones flew to Fairbanks to pick up replacement parts and returned to drop them within a few hours. Robbins quickly repaired the landing gear and was able to depart later that day for Fairbanks. Deteriorating snow conditions would not allow him to take off with the additional weight of passengers, so he was forced to leave the climbers behind. Olton and Spadavecchia decided to try to hike out on their own, and they made it safely.

No more planes landed on Mount McKinley that season, or for several years. One last flight over the mountain that summer seems ironic in retrospect. In August, while a climbing party was retrieving Theodore Koven's body from Muldrow Glacier, Joe Crosson flew high overhead and scattered the ashes of a Texas man. The man had struck it rich in the Alaska gold fields and wished his final resting place to be on the slopes of Mount McKinley. Crosson was honoring the wishes of a man who wanted to spend eternity on the mountain, while the climbers below struggled to free a comrade from the same fate.

Joe with Slim Williams

16

JOINING THE PAN AM SYSTEM

Fairbanks, summer 1932. As chief pilot for Alaskan Airways, Joe Crosson was using his knowledge and skill in the northern sky to make air travel safe and widely available in the Territory. Alaskan Airways was the realization of the desire by Crosson, Ben Eielson, and George King to create a dependable regional airline. But by no means had the transition from frontier operation to reliable air carrier been easy.

Gone were the ancient OX-5, Hisso, and Hispana-Suiza motors. The early water-cooled motors were cantankerous and undependable. Cooling systems leaked and froze in the cold. Soft bearings and weak valves required continuous maintenance, and they routinely failed. The Alaskan Airways fleet was now equipped with modern radial engines. The Wasp engines from Pratt & Whitney and Wright Whirlwind engines, soon to be legendary for their dependability, were welcomed by pilots, mechanics, and passengers alike.

Compared with Alaskan Airways' new state-of-the-art cabin monoplanes, the planes Crosson had flown in San Diego and in the Territory just six years earlier were frail and primitive. The biplanes

August 1932

U.S. Weather Bureau successfully transmits weather maps between Cleveland and Washington, D.C., using a teletype.

◄ *Joe Crosson shakes hands with Slim Williams who was promoting a highway to Alaska by riding a motorcycle to the continental United States. The Electra was used to haul gear for him.*

169

that remained in the Alaskan Airways fleet were relatively modern craft, but even these were being phased out.

Still, things were far from perfect. Growth of the airline had been financially expensive and emotionally troubling. Russ Merrill and Ben Eielson both died in crashes during the start-up days. The search for Eielson was rumored to have cost the company the enormous sum of fifty thousand dollars. Small mishaps with the airplanes were still regular occurrences. Although great strides had been made to improve aviation in Alaska, dependability was still compromised by primitive communications, a lack of airports, marginal runways, and inadequate weather reporting.

American Airways and its parent company, the Aviation Corporation of America, had weathered the expensive years of building Alaskan Airways into a dependable flying operation in Alaska without ever realizing a profit. Constructing runways and maintaining planes, offices, and hangars at the widely separated terminals in Anchorage, Nome, and Fairbanks consumed all the revenue. Forced landings, although less common than earlier, were still a fact of life, and added greatly to operating expenses. By the summer of 1932 the finances of American Airways and the determination of its leaders had been stretched thin.

Rumors of major changes at Alaskan Airways had bubbled through the Territory for months. Warren Oakes, the American Airways executive in charge of the Alaska operation, was a good friend of Crosson's. He had stayed and hunted at Crosson's Mount Hayes hunting camp in the Alaska Range. The men trusted each other and were straightforward in their communications about what was happening with Alaskan Airways.

In one letter Crosson told Oakes about problems Alaskan Airways was experiencing due to increased competition:

> The annual court has been in session in Fairbanks for the last few weeks. Alaskan Airways succeeded in bringing most of the thirty odd witnesses from McGrath and Takotna, but we have encountered a great deal of trouble in getting them to return with us, as there is

an airplane for nearly every passenger. Today, Barnhill, Barrows, Munson, Bill Graham, Vic Ross, Percy Hubbard and Deiderley, besides an Alaskan Airways plane were waiting for the three or four passengers that were ready to return, so you see competition is keen.

About one increasingly cutthroat operator Joe wrote:

They will take you any place in the territory for fifty dollars or what have you and will cut in half any price that anyone else will

▲ *Mechanic Jim Hutchison (left) and pilots Robbie Robbins, Jerry Jones, and Ed Young worked for Pacific Alaska Airways and were among the friends of Joe Crosson.*

make. People think he is doing real well because he is doing so much flying, but if he is making money it is from bootlegging and handling "hot fur." He seems to be doing a very good business hauling liquor into Anchorage from some stills across the inlet.

In another letter, Crosson told Oakes about a series of recent mishaps involving Alaskan Airways:

Jerry had a forced landing with the Stinson, the cam drive gear went out and he landed on the side of a hill near Candle and Deering. He had three passengers but got the ship down okay and it was several days before we got parts over to him. . . . Blunt and Niemenen were both forced down with Wasp (engine) failure. Blunt landed fifteen miles from Fairbanks on the Tanana River. The Wasp swallowed a valve and wrecked the whole power section so had to take another engine down by dog team to get the plane out. The same day with in an hour of the time Blunt was forced down Niemenen was forced down about fifteen miles from Anchorage, a tooth broke off the cam drive pinion gear and went through the oil pump, and it looked as if he was trying to get into Anchorage with no oil pressure. He says not but the engine shows signs of having run without oil for some time, anyway we had to fly another engine down and install it, which meant a lot of work.

The responding letter from Oakes did little to mask the growing frustrations in New York:

> Your letter does not give a complimentary report of our operation, in fact, it sounds like one forced landing after another with equipment which is supposed to be in excellent shape and well maintained, while on the other hand, it appears competitors with no overhaul facilities and poor equipment have been doing a swell job. . . . I cannot see how we can possibly continue much longer, or rather I should put it this way—that I cannot see why we should continue much longer.

Something had to happen soon. Oakes and Crosson considered at least three possibilities.

One idea called for American Airways to purchase Pacific International Airlines, a small carrier based in Anchorage. PIA had an important revenue source, mail delivery contracts. By combining mail contracts and establishing regular schedules, Crosson believed profitability could be achieved.

A second idea called for Crosson and fellow Alaskan Airways pilot Ed Young to purchase the company and try to make a go of it on their own. Due to the increasingly competitive nature of flying in Alaska, this was a long shot.

▼ *The fleet of planes owned by Alaskan Airways before it became part of Pacific Alaska Airways included (from left) two Fairchild 71's, a Stinson Standard SB-1, a cabin Swallow, two new Standard D-25's, and a Stearman C2B. The last plane in the line is a Waco 9 that was owned by pilot and mechanic Freddie Moller.*

"A territory where people pay four hundred dollars for the privilege of walking behind a dogsled for ninety days is a good prospect for an airline."

The third possibility (and probably the most popular in the corporate boardroom) was to find a company that was interested in expanding into Alaska aviation and would purchase Alaskan Airways outright, taking American Airways completely out of the picture.

It was this third possibility that came to pass.

~

THE NEXT CHAPTER in modern Alaska aviation began with a press release from New York. Pan American Airways announced it had purchased Alaskan Airways, buying it outright from American Airways. Within days, Pan Am also bought Pacific International Airways (PIA). Both Alaska companies were merged in the summer of 1932 to create Pacific Alaska Airways (PAA), a subsidiary of Pan Am.

Pan American Airways was owned by Juan Trippe, a man who dreamed of an airline that encompassed the world. He started building his empire in 1927 with flights between Florida and Cuba. Early on, Trippe identified Alaska as a key piece in the world aviation puzzle. He formed a paper company, Alaska Air Transport, intent on eventually entering the air mail business in the Territory. This venture never materialized. But a remark by Trippe hinted at his plans: "A territory where people pay four hundred dollars for the privilege of walking behind a dogsled for ninety days is a good prospect for an airline."

Trippe's eventual move into Alaska aviation was, in part, based on information from Charles Lindbergh. During 1931, Charles and Anne Lindbergh flew across the top of Canada and Alaska and across the Bering Straits to Russia and Asia. Their craft was equipped with a Pan American radio set and supported by Trippe. Lindbergh's report to Trippe was positive about the possibility of establishing a route across the Arctic.

By 1933, Trippe's routes tied the United States to South America, the West Indies, Central America, Mexico, and Alaska. Establishing Pan Am in Alaska through Pacific Alaska Airways gave Trippe the opportunity to link the United States with Asia through Alaska and Siberia, if and when routes became available. This was Trippe's

primary motive in bringing Pan American to Alaska. In the meantime, his secondary plan was to strengthen the line within the Territory, which supported Crosson's dream of a strong airline connecting all of Alaska.

Staff assignments in the newly formed Pacific Alaska Airways held some surprises. In six years, Crosson had risen from the least experienced pilot to the most experienced in the Territory. He had been chief pilot of Alaskan Airways and had been named general manager before its purchase by Pan American. However, leadership positions in the new company were decided in New York.

When the two small regional airlines were bought and merged into Pacific Alaska Airways, pilots and mechanics from both companies were retained. Crosson had been in Alaska's skies considerably longer than the other men—Ed Young, Robbie Robbins, Jerry Jones, Matt Niemenen, Harry Blunt, and Joe Barrows—and he had been a respected leader in the larger of the two regional airlines.

▲ *Repair shops in the spacious Weeks Field hangar built in Fairbanks by Pacific Alaska Airways were the finest in Alaska. In the machine shop, mechanics could build special fittings for skis and carry out all types of repairs.*

▲ *A Fairchild 71 on wheels lies partially fallen through the ice on Harding Lake, south of Fairbanks. Pilots often landed on the lake ice on wheels long after winter had ended, sometimes leading to mishaps such as this when long, sunny days softened the ice.*

To the surprise of pilots and mechanics from Alaskan Airways, Crosson was appointed chief pilot, while Joe Barrows, a brash pilot from the second and smaller company, was named operations manager. This decision was not popular with most of the staff, but Crosson was a team player. He knew PAA was good for Alaska and was determined to help it succeed.

Crosson flew to Juneau to meet Lyman Peck, the new general manager of PAA. Peck, an experienced airline executive but new to Alaska, flew with Crosson to the regional offices in Anchorage, Nome, and Fairbanks to check out company assets and equipment. During the tour, several questions about the new airline were answered.

PAA would be headquartered in Fairbanks. Peck stated, "A line from the States is not in the immediate picture. We will work toward linking Alaska with existing air lines in the States but do not intend to do so immediately."

Peck's visions for the future were exciting to Crosson. "We have confidence in the future of Alaska," Peck told him. He announced plans for a two-way radio communication system, to be installed right away. Calling the system "essential to safe operation," Peck said it would be coordinated with the weather information being supplied by the U.S. Signal Corps.

Pacific Alaska Airways owned seven Fairchild 71 airplanes, two Stinsons, and one model each of the Fairchild 51, Stearman, Waco, Travel Air, Standard, Bellanca, Zenith, and Swallow. It was an odd fleet, but the largest ever assembled in Alaska.

With the financial backing of the corporation in New York, things began to change rapidly. Three new Fairchild 71's were flown to Alaska through Canada along with four new spare Pratt & Whitney Wasp radial engines. The entire fleet was painted in the new company's colors: black fuselage and orange wings. Plans were made to sell some of the older airplanes.

PAA inherited seven widely scattered mail contracts in the Interior and on the Alaska and Kenai Peninsulas from the companies they purchased. Mail contracts were set up in an unusual way that reduced profits for airlines. The routes had been designed to be run by dog teams for about half the year, when snow covered the way, and by riverboats for about half the year, when the waterways were free of ice. As a result, contracts were issued twice per year. Although airplanes could deliver mail less expensively than dog teams, they could not compete economically with wood-fired riverboats, which could haul tons of freight along with the mail. Therefore, PAA owned only winter-season mail contracts, and flying in summer was limited to air charters.

Alaska charter flying was very new to Pan American. The company was involved for the first time in operations routine to the Alaska bush: doctors flew to patients too sick to be moved, fur buyers hired planes to go from village to village to do their buying, miners moved supplies and equipment to remote locations.

In October 1932, Bob Gleason was hired to establish the radio communications system. Crosson recommended Gleason for the position. He trusted Gleason totally, a respect earned during the bleak Siberian winter when Gleason ran communications on the *Nanuk* during the search for Ben Eielson.

Although airplanes could deliver mail less expensively than dog teams, they could not compete economically with wood-fired riverboats, which could haul tons of freight along with the mail.

Along with his management duties, Crosson continued to do what he loved best: fly. And when the need arose he still went to the aid of others.

After the excitement of the purchase and merger settled down, a problem with Joe Barrows' leadership became apparent. The pilots and mechanics at PAA headquarters in Fairbanks had the utmost confidence and trust in Joe Crosson, but they didn't hold the same respect for Barrows. Crosson was easygoing and led by example. Gleason said Crosson "never asked anyone to do anything he wouldn't." Barrows on the other hand was gruff and demanding. A skilled pilot, he was unable to earn respect with his rough leadership style.

Gleason tells what happened next: "We weren't satisfied with Joe Barrows and someone originated a letter. . . . It was signed by everyone including me saying we wanted Joe Crosson to be the operations manager."

There was no telling how the mutinous move would be taken at corporate headquarters in New York. To everyone's surprise the solution came swiftly. Joe Crosson was appointed operations manager, and Joe Barrows went back to flying.

In December 1932, Pacific Alaska Airways advertised the first scheduled passenger flights in the Territory of Alaska. Alaskans could now plan on regular air travel over 2,500 miles of routes to the Yukon River drainage as far north as Wiseman in the Brooks Range, to Bristol Bay, Bethel, Anchorage, the Kenai Peninsula, Nome, and numerous villages.

Bob Gleason first installed transmitters and receivers at Fairbanks and in one of the Fairchild 71 planes, and he and Crosson inaugurated radio service. The system used by PAA employed Morse code, not voice transmission. Joe was new to code, but was able to receive and transmit on the round-trip flight to Nulato. One of the messages that Bob, an expert at code, received from Joe was, "Please not so fast."

Along with his management duties, Crosson continued to do what he loved best: fly. And when the need arose he still went to the aid of others. One call came in the darkest days of January 1933 when an old-timer named Van Bibber became seriously ill in his cabin seventy-five miles from Fairbanks on a remote stretch of the Wood River. Bob Buzby, a young dog musher, reported the old trapper needed immediate rescue.

Quickly a Fairchild was pushed out of the hangar and Crosson warmed the motor in temperatures that hit 50 below zero. Taking off in the ice fog that enveloped Weeks Field, Crosson, the musher, and a local doctor headed to the cabin. In an hour Joe was circling, looking for a place to land. He found a good stretch of snow about three-quarters of a mile upstream, in tight quarters with spruce trees at both ends.

Crosson brought the big Fairchild in over the trees and glided onto the powdery snow covering the river ice. The doctor and musher soon brought Van Bibber to the plane. Joe had no trouble getting the Fairchild back in the air and above the trees.

Once again over Fairbanks, Crosson set up his descent based on landmarks that peeked up through the fog. The plane slipped down into the soupy whiteness, but Joe's instinctive sense of direction was on target and the Fairchild touched down safely. Van Bibber recovered to spend many days back in his Wood River home.

Crosson warmed the motor in temperatures that hit 50 below zero. Taking off in the ice fog that enveloped Weeks Field, Crosson, the musher, and a local doctor headed to the cabin.

Will Rogers on the wing and Wiley Post signing autographs

17

DEATH AT BARROW

August 1935. Wiley Post's trip to Alaska in 1935 was a national event. He was traveling with America's folk hero, Will Rogers, a quick-thinking, sharp-witted spokesman for the working class. Popular as both movie star and newspaper columnist, Will Rogers related to the average citizen, and claimed "I never met a man I didn't like." Wiley Post and Will Rogers were both Oklahoma boys and the best of friends. Will was a great promoter of aviation and had absolute faith in Wiley's skill as a pilot, telling one reporter, "He's sure a marvelous flyer. I'll fly anywhere with him, if he'll take me along."

Joe and Lillian had been vacationing in California when Wiley confided to Joe that he planned to fly Will Rogers around the world, following his solo route in reverse. He wanted to introduce Will to the Crossons and spend time with them in Alaska.

Post and Rogers flew north in August 1935. Wiley no longer flew his famous *Winnie Mae*. Instead they traveled in a bright red craft of his own design. Post's odd plane was actually a combination of several airplanes. A Lockheed Orion fuselage was mated to an experimental Lockheed Explorer wing. In Seattle the plane was fitted with floats from a Fairchild 71 on loan from Pacific Alaska Airways. The 550-horsepower supercharged Wasp radial motor and three-bladed

August 20, 1935 Boeing 299 (prototype of the B-17, the Flying Fortess bomber of World War II) flies 2,100 miles nonstop between Seattle and Washington, D.C.

◄ *Wiley Post signs autographs for Fairbanks kids who followed him and Will Rogers to the Chena River float where Post's plane was tied.*

▲ Will Rogers, on the wing, and Wiley Post in the cockpit talk with Joe Crosson (lower right) after landing on the Chena River in Fairbanks on August 12, 1935.

adjustable-pitch propeller had never been fitted to either of the Lockheed models. The low-wing craft that Wiley put together was constructed without the aid of an aeronautical engineer. The resulting configuration was both nose heavy and overpowered.

Leaving Seattle's Lake Union with Will aboard, Wiley maneuvered his unusual bird through low clouds, mist, forested islands, and coastal mountains. Sometimes flying well below one hundred feet to stay below the overcast, he guided the plane through the numerous islands and channels on the way north. Wiley landed the plane in Gastineau Channel at Juneau and taxied to the seaplane dock. He was back in Alaska.

Joe Crosson was there to greet his friend, but he wasn't alone. Territorial officials and hundreds of well-wishers swarmed over the dock to welcome the famous pair. As the cockpit opened, Wiley spotted his pal and pointed him out to Will. Rogers waved and the first words out of his mouth were "Hi Joe!" Joe chuckled, honored but slightly embarrassed.

Crosson took the visitors to a banquet at the governor's mansion

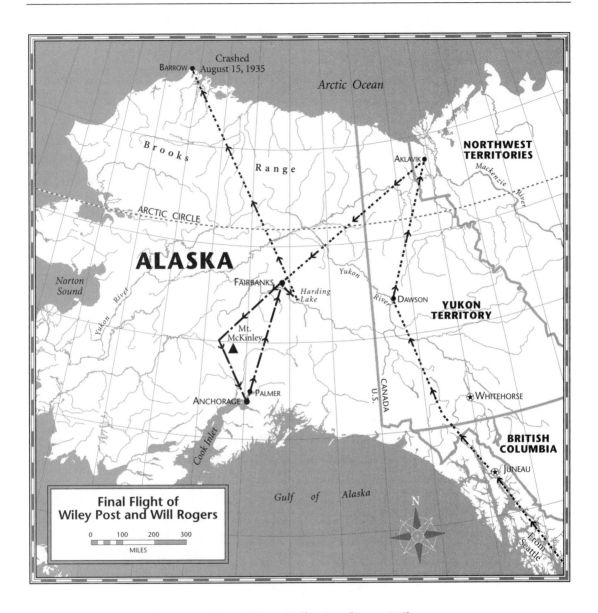

Final Flight of
Wiley Post and Will Rogers

0   100   200   300
MILES

hosted by Territorial Governor John W. Troy. Following dinner, Wiley
and Will greeted the people of Juneau during a live radio broadcast on
local station KINY. Wiley, remembering his last round-the-world flight
and Joe's help, told the audience,

"I've always liked this country and always had a good time here,
except when I broke down and got lost on my trip around the world,

"Wiley and I are like a couple of country boys in an old Ford: we don't know where we are going and we don't care."

and even then there was a good friend to come along and pull me out of it."

Always the good-natured entertainer, Rogers flattered his audience, saying, "I have never been here before and I ought to be ashamed of myself. It ought to be in the Constitution that everybody had to come here." He didn't, however, disclose their plans to fly around the world. Instead he claimed they were drifting about on a vacation: "Wiley and I are like a couple of country boys in an old Ford: we don't know where we are going and we don't care."

The following day was spent enjoying Juneau, shopping for wet-weather clothes and souvenirs, and wandering around the city in the drizzling rain. After a long day the group returned to the Gastineau Hotel, where Will, Wiley, and Joe stayed up late, outdoing each other in storytelling, laughing and talking.

At one point Joe told a colorful story he had heard about Will's good friend Rex Beach. Rex had been north during the gold rush, and stories of his adventures lingered. The three men were surprised and delighted when the famous author coincidentally walked into the Gastineau Hotel that night and joined in the hilarity. Much to Joe's chagrin, Will made him tell the story again.

Will Rogers traveled with a portable typewriter, and each day he wrote a column sharing his personal perspective on Alaska. Newspapers across the country followed Will and Wiley in their travels.

From Juneau the two men flew north to Aklavik at the top of Canada, and returned to Alaska the following day. Crosson flew directly back to Fairbanks to help prepare for their arrival in that city.

~

THE LATE-SUMMER day dawned bright, but with a chill that warned of the approaching fall. It was early afternoon when Wiley Post buzzed Fairbanks in the big floatplane to announce their arrival and then landed on the Chena River, just outside of town at Spencer's Homestead. Joe directed Wiley to the floatplane dock. The door opened and Fairbanks got its first glimpse of a famous movie star. Will Rogers called out, "Want a rope, Joe?" Joe tied the plane to the dock as

Will joked, "Is that all the river you got? Gotta have more river than that for an airplane."

The riverbank was alive with well-wishers. More than seventy-five cars made the mile-and-a-half trip from downtown to the dock, where the brilliant red plane offered a striking contrast to the murky brown water and the green willows and grasses lining the bank. Joe's new Chrysler led an impromptu parade back to downtown Fairbanks. Lillian held the new baby, Don, and Joe Jr. as she rode with her husband and the famous Oklahomans.

▲ *Will Rogers jokes with Joe Crosson Jr. as proud father Joe looks on.*

Will Rogers wanted to meet the local sourdoughs, and he and Wiley chose to stay at the Pioneer Hotel. Wiley relaxed with Joe during the afternoon while Will took an impromptu self-guided walking tour of the town. He casually wandered the street and attracted a parade of local children, like the Pied Piper. As always, he was at ease in his surroundings.

A Crosson home-cooked meal was in order. Lillian cooked a special recipe, veal and pork shaped and fried like chicken. Will, teasing her about her "chicken legs," made himself at home and even helped mash the potatoes. Over dinner the Crossons enlightened their visitors with talk of Alaska and things they should see while there. The subject turned to Barrow at the top of the world. Lillian's description of Charlie Brower, who was nicknamed King of the Arctic, intrigued Rogers. Brower was a colorful trader who had gone to Barrow on a whaling ship and had been there for decades, longer than any white man before him. Will decided he wanted to meet Charlie, who would no doubt be an excellent subject for his newspaper columns. Plans were made to include Barrow on the trip.

The morning of August 15
found Barrow at 45 degrees
Fahrenheit in a dense fog—
very poor flying conditions.

Joe shifted into tour guide mode. He took Will and Wiley out to the Hi-Yu mine, in which he and Lillian were partners with other miners. Over the next days, he flew the guests to the Matanuska Colony, where farmers were cultivating grains and vegetables, and to Mount McKinley National Park. Will Rogers wrote of the trip around McKinley:

> Well, we had a day off today and nothing to do, so we went flying with friend Joe Crosson, Alaska's crack pilot, who is a great friend of Wiley's and helped him on his difficulties up here on his record trips. In a Lockheed Electra we scaled Mount McKinley, the highest one on the American continent. Bright, sunny and the most beautiful sight I ever saw . . . Crosson has landed on a glacier over half way up it in a plane and took off.

Wiley was getting serious about spending more time in Alaska. He wanted to try mining and do more hunting. On the same day he and Will left for Barrow, Wiley went house hunting. Lillian remembered the day: "Joe and Wiley rented a house from Harry Avakoff the morning Wiley left so Wiley and his wife Mae could come back to live and Wiley could go wolf hunting." When the trip with Will was finished, Wiley would move to Fairbanks.

Barrow had a wireless radio station and a Signal Corps radioman to send weather reports to Fairbanks. The morning of August 15 found Barrow at 45 degrees Fahrenheit in a dense fog—very poor flying conditions. Wiley thought conditions might improve, so he got ready for the flight. The stretch of the Chena River near Fairbanks where Wiley had landed was too short to manage a takeoff with full fuel tanks. The adventurers flew fifty miles south to Harding Lake, which offered miles of smooth water and a safe takeoff with a full load of fuel.

"Wiley was anxious to leave but Joe was worried about the weather," Lillian said. "Joe offered to fly them up when the weather near Barrow improved, but Wiley would have no part of it. He wanted to make the trip himself."

Will had some last minute errands to complete, so Lillian drove him around Fairbanks. At the Lavery Store he picked up a watch he

◄ *Wiley Post consults with Joe in Juneau on a course to take him to Aklavik, Canada, before heading for Fairbanks.*

had dropped off for repairs. Lillian recalled that his casual nature did not change; he stopped in the middle of the street to talk with local people. At the grocery store he bought canned beans for the trip. At the federal building he took the elevator to an office where he could telegraph his wife.

Few people knew more about Alaska weather, or how bad it could get, than Joe Crosson. He encouraged Wiley to postpone the trip north. As a compromise, Wiley told Joe that after refueling at Harding Lake, he would go to the roadhouse a few miles from the lake and phone Joe for current weather conditions at Barrow. If the weather was getting worse, he would postpone the flight.

The weather at Barrow did get worse, but the promised call from Wiley never came. Wiley left without calling Joe.

∼

THAT EVENING, at a hunting camp near Barrow, Eskimo hunter Claire Okpeaha listened intently. It was after 6:00 p.m. Never in his years of hunting in the arctic had he heard such an unusual, distant droning. Surely it couldn't be an airplane on such a foggy and windy day. The

► *Will Rogers talks with a group of people on the streets of Fairbanks. Local children followed the good-natured humorist wherever he went, no doubt in part due to his reputation of handing out silver dollars.*

sound slowly grew louder, and a large, red floatplane emerged from the mist, circled the camp, and landed nearby on the Walapka River. The pilot, wearing a white eye-patch, emerged. The pilot and his jovial passenger climbed the embankment to the camp and the waiting Okpeaha family. Claire's wife and children stood by their tent and looked curiously at the unexpected visitors.

The men were lost. They were searching for Barrow, which was less than twenty miles away across the tundra. Claire pointed the way to the town. The men said good-bye and climbed back in the plane, and the air again reverberated with the sound of the big radial engine.

Heading into the wind, Wiley soon had the plane off the water in a climbing turn. At about fifty feet altitude, the motor sputtered and fell silent. At that low altitude, there was no time for corrective action. Watching from the embankment, the Okpeaha family froze in disbelief. The airplane slid sideways out of the air and crashed nose first in the lagoon on the edge of the river. With an impact sufficient to drive the motor back into the cabin, the plane came to rest upside down in a crumpled heap. The sickening chorus of shattering pieces was followed by an eerie quiet. The only sounds were the wind on the tundra and a faint sizzle from the hot steel of the engine cooling in the icy water.

The sickening chorus of shattering pieces was followed by an eerie quiet. The only sounds were the wind on the tundra and a faint sizzle from the hot steel of the engine cooling in the icy water.

Claire and his son waded toward the crash and called out, but there was no answer. Claire turned and began to run for help. He didn't stop until he reached Barrow. A message from radioman Stanley Morgan in Barrow soon traveled around the country.

The nation was stunned. Two of America's favorite sons were dead in the farthest reaches of arctic Alaska. Nowhere was the shock greater than in the Fairbanks home of Joe and Lillian Crosson.

The telephone startled them awake at 6:00 a.m. It was Joe Barrows, a pilot for Pacific Alaska Airways in Fairbanks. "I knew something was wrong," Lillian remembered. "I followed Joe to the kitchen. He answered the phone, listened in silence, hung up, steadied himself, and told me about the crash. Then he went into the bathroom and got physically ill. He recovered, came out and started gathering clothes and other gear to take with him on a flight to Barrow to retrieve the bodies."

Lillian knew how shocked Joe was, and the grief he felt. She begged him to find another pilot to take the trip, but the only other Alaska pilot who had ever flown to Barrow was Noel Wien, and he was in Nome.

Joe had the mechanics at PAA prepare a Fairchild 71 on floats for the long flight to Barrow. He stowed several five-gallon cans of aviation gas in the cabin for use in refueling along the way. He also called Bob Gleason and asked him to come along as his radio officer.

Gleason remembered the flight to Barrow: "We started out and it wasn't too bad. We had a little trouble getting through the mountains."

*Joe returned to the plane
and, with the help of
villagers, loaded his sad
cargo: the bodies of his
friends. It was one of the
lowest moments of his life.*

Crosson tried a couple of passes before getting through the Brooks Range. Gleason was busy getting radio weather reports from Wiseman and Barrow, where the weather was not improving.

A wire came to Fairbanks from Charles Lindbergh, asking Crosson to fly to Barrow and retrieve the bodies. By the time the wire arrived, Crosson was already about halfway there.

Once through the mountains, Crosson landed the Fairchild on one of the thousands of unnamed lakes to refuel with Gleason's help. Gleason recalled the remaining flight to Barrow: "We go on into Barrow and it's really lousy weather, low clouds—drizzle—fog, but Joe knew Barrow very well and we went in and landed on the lagoon."

While Crosson went into the village, Gleason stayed with the plane to monitor the radio. It had taken eight hours to cover the five hundred miles from Fairbanks. Villagers brought gas, and Gleason refueled the plane. He also stowed twelve five-gallon cans of gas inside the plane for refueling on the return trip.

A group of local men had brought the bodies of Post and Rogers to Barrow by boat. Their injuries had been severe, and Dr. Henry Greist and Charlie Brower had worked through the night to realign limbs and suture the massive wounds. Joe returned to the plane and, with the help of villagers, loaded his sad cargo: the bodies of his friends. It was one of the lowest moments of his life.

Taxiing on the lagoon, Crosson hit a shallow gravel bar and the Fairchild stuck fast. Gleason got out and tied a rope to the tail, pulling back and forth while Crosson gunned the motor to work the plane off the bar. Once it was freed, they took off in bad weather and dangerous flying conditions for the return to Fairbanks.

In their years of flying together, Gleason always knew Crosson to be as careful as he was skilled. The pilot had a reputation for not taking unnecessary risks. But the burden of his personal loss and the responsibility he assumed to get the bodies home weighed heavily on Crosson. It was on the flight back to Fairbanks that Gleason saw him take big chances for the first time.

"I can remember flying in the Colville River," Gleason said. Crosson was staying down low in order to spot landmarks below the overcast and fog. "The banks aren't very high, probably 20 feet and I couldn't see over the banks. We were down on the river."

The weather was terrible, but Crosson kept trying to get back through the mountains. "I guess I was scared," Gleason said, "but I was worried that Joe was trying to do too much and how he felt about Post. That concerned me that he might be trying a little too hard."

Crosson was clearly feeling the strain. Throughout the flight, he hadn't spoken aloud about the crash or admitted the reason for the trip. It was as if he couldn't admit out loud that his friends were dead.

They pushed on with almost no visibility and made it through the Brooks Range. The Fairchild broke out into sunshine, and Crosson landed on Wild River Lake to refuel. During the refueling Joe first acknowledged what the flight was for—but in the most unusual way.

Gleason remembered the incident: "I'm up on top putting in the gas again and I hear a clank like wood against wood. I look out there and here's a guy in a little, I guess you'd call it a canoe made out of a sluice box. A sluice box with an outrigger on it, and he's paddling out to us."

When the prospector got near to the plane, he called out, "Are you Frank Pollock?"

"No," Joe answered.

"Well, Frank Pollock is supposed to be bringing my winter grub."

Joe told the prospector he would relay the message to Pollock in Fairbanks, and then told the prospector, "We've got the bodies of Post and Rogers here. We're taking them back to Fairbanks."

It was as if Crosson had told the prospector that he and Gleason were out for a pleasure flight. The man replied: "Well, when you get back to Fairbanks you tell Pollock I need my grub."

Lillian waited at the PAA radio shack at Weeks Field for word of her husband. Radio officer Chuck Huntley finally told her, "Go home and rest, we'll call you when we hear from them." Later she learned that Huntley had lost contact with Joe, but didn't want her to know.

After refueling on the lake, Crosson and Gleason flew on to Fairbanks and landed on the Chena River right in town. The bodies were taken to the funeral home. Most of the dead men's personal effects had been dried out by the doctor in Barrow, but the contents of their

Throughout the flight, he hadn't spoken aloud about the crash or admitted the reason for the trip. It was as if he couldn't admit out loud that his friends were dead.

"We got a strange
message from them
signed 'Trippe' saying
we should land at
Vancouver—not
Seattle," Gleason said.
"We wondered why the
hell they wanted us to
land at Vancouver
instead of Seattle."

wallets were still wet. Lillian dried the contents by the cookstove, where two days earlier she had prepared the men's last home-cooked meal.

As she removed the items from Will Rogers' wallet, one by one Lillian recognized the family photos he had showed her at the Model Cafe just a day or two before. Will had proudly pulled out the pictures and identified each family member. "He was very sentimental when he looked at the picture of his daughter, a budding actress," Lillian said. "I think I may have reminded him of his daughter. He was very fatherly to me and kind to little Joe." This time the pictures made her cry.

After the flight, Joe was exhausted. "Joe looked like he'd aged ten years," Lillian said.

~

WHILE JOE RESTED, Pacific Alaska Airways mechanics prepared a Lockheed Electra for the flight to Seattle. The Electra was the most modern plane flying in Alaska in 1935—an all-metal, twin-engine craft with partially retractable landing gear and two-position propellers. The plane was fitted with a fuel tank in the cabin so that gas carried in five-gallon cans could be added to the tank in flight.

When the plane was ready, the remains of Wiley Post and Will Rogers were placed inside. Joe Crosson, co-pilot Bill Knox, and radio flight officer Bob Gleason climbed in. They flew to Whitehorse, Yukon Territory, where they refueled and then left for a planned nonstop flight to Seattle.

Nearing Prince George, British Columbia, in perfect flying weather, Gleason received a transmission from the Pan American office in Oakland, California. "We got a strange message from them signed 'Trippe' saying we should land at Vancouver—not Seattle," Gleason said. "We wondered why the hell they wanted us to land at Vancouver instead of Seattle." But Juan Trippe was the owner of Pan American Airways, parent company of Pacific Alaska Airways, and their boss. Crosson landed at Vancouver.

On the ground, Crosson was directed to taxi the plane into a hangar, and the hangar doors were closed and locked. The three flyers were taken to the home of a friend of Trippe to await further instructions. In the morning, they received a phone call telling them what time to arrive in Seattle. Crosson followed instructions and arrived in the skies above Seattle on schedule.

Joe handled his grief personally, not sharing it even with his closest friends or family.

An Army plane intercepted them outside Seattle and escorted them to Boeing Field. Navy planes also flew nearby in salute to the fallen men. The Lockheed Electra touched down at the field, where about fifteen thousand people waited to see the plane carrying Wiley Post and Will Rogers on their final trip. Again, Crosson's plane was directed into a hangar, which was then closed and locked.

Gleaming on the tarmac next to where Crosson's plane was directed sat a shiny new DC-2, with Pan American painted in large, bright red letters on the side. Slowly Crosson and Gleason realized why they had been ordered to stop overnight in Vancouver. The DC-2, Trippe's newest and best-looking aircraft, had been in Texas. Trippe knew that newsreel cameras and photographers would document every aspect of the return of Post and Rogers, and he wanted his new plane with his company's logo in the pictures.

"They didn't want us to get to Seattle until the Pan Am DC-2 from Texas could get up to Seattle," Gleason said. Juan Trippe had made thousands of people at the airfield and millions around the world wait an extra day while he set up a publicity stunt. Crosson was deeply troubled by the incident.

The bodies were transferred to the DC-2 and another crew flew them to Burbank, California, where Will Rogers' funeral was held. The plane then continued on to Oklahoma, where Wiley Post was buried. News reports featured Crosson's great effort in returning the bodies of Post and Rogers, and he received letters of thanks from people across the country.

The loss of his friends and the trip to recover their bodies deeply affected Joe, but his outward behavior did not betray his feelings. Joe handled his grief personally, not sharing it even with his closest friends or family. Lillian recalled, "He wasn't the type to talk much about it. Joe was very quiet and kept it all inside, but he really suffered a loss with Wiley, much like he did with Marvel."

Zelma and Esler

18

GOLD FEVER

Gold country, 1935. The death of Wiley Post was a severe blow to Joe. Wiley had shared more than Joe's love for flying and the outdoors. The pilot from Oklahoma had also planned to join in the mining ventures that occupied much of the Crossons' spare time. Joe was now active in two large gold mining operations in the Interior.

The Mastodon Mining Company on Deadwood Creek, in the Circle Mining District, was situated about a hundred miles north of Fairbanks, in rolling, mostly treeless, tundra-covered hills. Water from Deadwood Creek eventually finds the Yukon River, even farther to the north.

The Crossons' Mastodon Mining venture was a placer gold mine typical of the era in Alaska. Caterpillar tractors were used to scrape away several feet of overburden—the plants and organic layer that covered the underlying gravel and other material, where the gold hides near bedrock. With the rich ground exposed, a large dragline scooped it up and loaded it into a series of separators and sluice boxes. At that point, water from the creek was pumped at high pressure through the sluice boxes, which are descending steel chutes two or three feet wide and up to thirty feet long, with sides about eighteen inches high. If everything is set up correctly, rocks, sand, and dirt wash out of the box and raw gold settles into the riffles on the bottom.

March 9, 1935

Hermann Goering announces the existence of a German Air Force, breaking terms agreed to at the end of World War I in the Treaty of Versailles.

◄ *Life at the Hi-Yu was a family affair. Joe's younger sister Zelma worked as the camp cook and his father Esler, a skilled woodworker, was constantly busy on projects around the mine.*

He was always grubstaking the prospectors, and I never knew who would turn up at the house looking for him. He trusted all of the old prospectors and they all looked up to him.

The Crossons' other operation was Joe's favorite, and very much a family endeavor. The Hi-Yu mine, twenty miles north of Fairbanks, was one of the largest hard-rock gold mines in the region. Hard-rock miners locate veins of gold in quartz rock and dig tunnels to follow the vein. The rock is drilled, blasted loose with explosives, and removed in ore cars to a dump for stockpiling. The miners follow the vein up, down, and deeper into the mountain until it plays out and is lost. Rock in the dump is worked into a powder to extract the gold.

Specialized equipment was needed at the Hi-Yu. A stamp mill, largest in the district, was installed to crush the rock, and a large diesel plant supplied power to the whole operation. The large metal hammers of the mining stamps pound the rocks until they are crushed into a fine powder. This crushed ore is washed on shaker tables and combined with mercury, which bonds to the gold and forms a gray, pastelike substance called an amalgam. The amalgam is then smelted, or cooked, which draws off the mercury and leaves the liquid gold, which is poured into molds and cooled to form ingots.

Joe developed an interest in mining soon after arriving in Alaska. Many of the local prospectors counted on Joe and other good-hearted Alaskans to grubstake their ventures—providing the food and supplies they needed for months of living on remote creeks while they searched for gold. If the prospector made a find, a claim was filed and the miner and his benefactor became partners. More often than not, no gold was found and the prospector ended up looking for another grubstake.

Lillian remembered Joe's concern for the old-timers. "Joe was always generous. He was always grubstaking the prospectors, and I never knew who would turn up at the house looking for him. He trusted all of the old prospectors and they all looked up to him. They were always polite and welcome at the house. Many times they joined us for dinner."

Joe's old friend Ernie Franzen got him interested in the hard-rock mine. Ernie, a skilled mechanic, prospector, and miner, was an old-timer who had narrowly avoided death with Joe years earlier. It was Ernie who had risked his life while shielding Joe from flames in the burning Standard airplane while Joe made an emergency landing on a frozen lake in 1926. The pair had watched helplessly as the craft burned and spent the next arduous days on the trail hiking out. Joe trusted Ernie's judgment as a miner and welcomed the chance to join him in a venture. Eventually a partnership between Franzen, Crosson, and fellow PAA pilot Ed Young was formed to develop the property. They were later joined by a mining man named Don Gustafason.

Lillian Crosson suggested the partners name their company "Hi-Yu," the original name for the property. The term was thought to be an Indian expression for "heap big," and the partners hoped the mine would hold "heap big" riches. As Lillian put it, the partners "knew gold was in the ground, but finding it was difficult." As it developed, the Hi-Yu became a large operation that involved much of the Crosson family.

▲ *The Hi-Yu gold mine in which the Crossons were among the partners was named by Lillian Crosson for a popular phrase meaning "heap big," in hopes the mine held "heap big" riches.*

Joe's parents Esler and Elizabeth were living part of the time at their home in San Diego and part of the time with Joe and Lillian and their grandchildren in Alaska. Joe's younger sister, Zelma, and her husband, Barney Frizell, had moved to Fairbanks. Esler, a skilled carpenter, moved out to the property to help with construction. Zelma and Barney also moved to the mine and became the camp cooks, living in a wall tent not far from the cookhouse. Zelma, displaying her trademark Crosson smile, was cheerful and alive with chatter as she hurried about making the miners feel at home.

When time allowed, Joe gathered Lillian and the boys and drove the family along the long, dusty road from Fairbanks, up Cleary Summit, and down the Fairbanks Creek road to the Hi-Yu. Joe worked with the crew while Lillian and the boys spent sunny summer days hiking, picking berries, and panning for gold. Lillian loved to pan for

▲ At the Hi-Yu, gold-bearing ore was mined underground and taken to the surface on small ore cars. From there it was taken to a stamp mill, a crushing operation that pulverized the rock before the gold was extracted.

gold in the bubbling creeks well into the evening. As she put it, "Something about it gets in your blood." The mine was Joe's playground. Intricate machinery appealed to his mechanical nature, and he loved working with the generators, the ten-stamp mill, and the drills, ore cars, and other equipment.

Evenings found all coming together in the cookhouse as Barney rang the dinner bell and Zelma served up heaping portions to the crew of miners who lived in the bunkhouse and numbered more than a dozen at the peak of operation. Hungry visitors were also welcomed by Zelma's cheerful greeting, Barney's firm handshake, and the smell of fresh-baked bread and pie.

Joe proudly showed the Hi-Yu operation to friends, including Wiley Post and Will Rogers. Rogers wrote about his trip to the Hi-Yu and about an incident involving the Crossons' dog Mickey. Rogers had heard the story from Ernie Franzen and wrote it down for his column:

Joe Crosson, the ace pilot that we were with so much in Fairbanks, an old friend of Wiley's, has a mine, and we went out there, and he has a partner, a Swedish fellow that runs it, and he had just killed a bear right at his house door, the Swedish fellow tells how Mickey went out one night and run the bear in. Well, as a matter of fact, Mickey went out and the bear chased him in, and Ernest had to shoot the bear to keep him from running Mickey under the bed.

The Hi-Yu operated until World War II. During the war, the government decided that gold mining was not vital to the war effort and shut down the nation's gold mines. After the moratorium was lifted, conditions were never right to start the operation again. The mine changed hands without rendering a profit to any of the original partners. But many years later, at the turn of the twenty-first century, the Hi-Yu property became part of one of the largest gold mining complexes in North America. Joe and his partners were in the right place, but at the wrong time.

▼ Miners clean gold out of a sluice box at the Mastodon Mining Company, another mining operation in which the Crossons were partners.

JOE CROSSON. Alaska's Mercy Flyer. In addition to his regular job of flying the frozen Northland, Crosson always finds time to aid the needy. Flights with serum and medicine to isolated communities . . . successful search for the body of his aviator friend, Carl Ben Eielson . . . combing the wastes of the Arctic for the lost Russian flyers . . . returning the bodies of Will Rogers and Wiley Post to grief-stricken America—these are a few of the exploits which have earned him the title of "Mercy Flyer." Manages Alaska Service of Pan American Airways.

Joe Crosson stamp

19

POPULAR HERO

1936. The daring men and women who pushed aviation to the limits were popular heroes. They seemed to live a life of excitement that few Americans could ever do more than dream about. Soaring through clouds, setting records, and swooping out of the sky in thrilling rescues, the pilots were always in the public eye—even when the stories were exaggerated or inaccurate. It didn't matter. Pilots were looked up to, and across America children gazed skyward at every passing plane, dreaming of the day they would take the controls.

During the 1930s, newspapers across the United States sponsored an organization that fostered this dream, the Junior Birdmen. The Seattle Wing of the Junior Birdmen had more than eight thousand members in 1936, and some other cities had even larger chapters. Junior Birdmen had their own song, sponsored model-building contests, issued pilot's wings to the young members, and generally promoted aviation to future pilots.

The Junior Birdmen also conducted an annual popularity poll in the sponsoring newspapers, in which the various Wings voted for their favorite pilots. Crosson never won the poll, but his name was always entered alongside the likes of Eddie Rickenbacker, Charles Lindbergh, Amelia Earhart, Jimmy Doolittle, and Howard Hughes by some of the

October 21, 1936

Pan American Airways inaugurates weekly service between San Francisco and Manila with the four-engine flying boat Hawaiian Clipper.

◀ *Patrons of Skelly Oil were presented a stamp featuring Joe Crosson to add to an Air Heroes album that included Amelia Earhart, Wiley Post, and Jimmy Doolittle.*

▲ *True Comics served up a flamboyant version of Joe Crosson's exploits in Alaska.*

would-be pilots who made up the ranks of the Junior Birdmen.

An article about the poll in a Seattle newspaper said "Crosson's exploits and daring are well known to all followers of aviation." He was identified as a "veteran Alaskan flyer, famous for many rescue flights. Flew bodies of Post and Rogers from Point Barrow, Alaska."

Crosson's fame also got him featured on a radio show hosted by Roscoe Turner, a flamboyant race pilot and a tireless champion of flying. This self-appointed colonel flew across the United States, sharing the cockpit with his lion cub Gilmore and promoting flying wherever he could. In 1940, Turner parlayed his popularity into the radio series called *Skyblazers*.

The show was a radio melodrama, with each episode purporting to tell the story of an American pilot and his or her exploits. The show opened with airplane sounds while the announcer proclaimed, "The makers of Wonder Bread present *Skyblazers*, based on the adventures of the men and women who pioneered new trails in the sky, that we might fly."

One *Skyblazers* program featured Joe Crosson—but the show stretched the truth very thin. Turner's spiel went like this: "Contact, *Skyblazers*, tonight I'm going to tell you the strange story of an aviator who, although he was the most hated man in Alaska, saved the lives of hundreds of people there. The story begins in San Diego, California, nineteen and twenty six, when Joe Crosson, then twenty three years old, was running a taxi service with his homemade airplane. . . . "

Turner's imagination and that of the writers went well beyond reality. In thirty minutes, Turner's story had Crosson being hated by the dogsled mail carriers and also rescuing a musher, proving the value of flying in Alaska. In between, the story included just about every feat Crosson had ever accomplished, and a few he hadn't.

Crosson as the nearly superhuman pilot surfaced again in 1941.

Issue number four of *True Comics* carried stories about General George C. Marshall, the American flag, Dolly Madison, Chiang Kai-shek, and Joe Crosson. In vivid color, Joe darted across the Alaskan sky, dodging mountain peaks and packs of wolves on his precarious journey to rescue starving reindeer herders stranded in the arctic wilderness. The truth about Crosson's accomplishments would have been enough to make a great story, but the writers and artists had their own idea of heroism.

Crosson was also a featured aviator in a series of stamps produced by Skelly Oil as a sales promotion. Among the other flyers depicted on the stamps were Amelia Earhart, Wiley Post, and Jimmy Doolittle.

Crosson emerged as a popular figure with people who followed flying. His mail regularly included letters from fans asking for his autograph. Always the gentleman, Joe complied, and he sometimes left signed letterhead stationery so his secretary could mail out replies in his absence.

Crosson's name and reputation for arctic adventure was also sought in advertising. After he appeared in a Camel cigarette advertisement, the company continued to send him a carton of cigarettes each month for years, despite the fact that he gave up smoking.

One man in Seattle sought Crosson's endorsement for a parka he had designed for extreme winter temperatures. Crosson offered some advice on the design. When it was finished, Crosson tried the parka and liked it.

An advertisement in the *Seattle Post-Intelligencer* featured a picture of Crosson wearing the goose-down parka designed by Eddie Bauer, and included the pilot's positive evaluation. The days of paid endorsements by well-known heroes of sports and adventure were far in the future. In fact, Joe insisted the ad carry a disclaimer stating that the evaluation was his alone, not that of Pacific Alaska Airways or Pan American, and that neither he nor the airlines received compensation for the endorsement. Until the 1980s, literature from the Eddie Bauer company stated that some of the outdoor gear had been used by Alaska bush pilot Joe Crosson.

▲ *Crosson was pictured on the cover of the November 1940 issue of New Horizons magazine as he was rising through the ranks of Pan American Airways.*

Joe with Pacific Alaska Airways pilots

20

BUILDING AN AIRLINE

Fairbanks, 1933-1935. Pan American faced a dilemma in Alaska. Their Pacific Alaska Airways pilots were clearly some of the most gifted aviators in the Pan American system—yet they were some of the least-qualified under the requirements dictated for pilots out of New York headquarters. Gifted as they were, the fur-clad bush pilots that Joe had assembled would have to change.

Pan American's standards for pilots were raised as the company expanded. When the Alaska operation was established, requirements for pilots were reaching their zenith. Pan Am pilots commanded respect in their crisp blue uniform, white shirt and tie, and cap, and the shiny wings emblem that designated their position. Pilots were required to master instrument flying, celestial navigation, and radio operation, including fluency in sending and receiving Morse code. College degrees were preferred. None of the Pacific Alaska Airways pilots could meet all the requirements.

Pan American's vice-president, Harold Bixby, summed up the feelings in New York:

> First thing, we've got to do something about the pilots up there. A lot of them are old-timers, and they've never had any instrument

September 13, 1935

Howard Hughes sets a land-plane speed record of 352 miles per hour in California.

◄ *Proud pilots pose with a Pacific Alaska Airways Lockheed Electra. They are (from left) Joe Crosson, Murray Stewart, Robbie Robbins, Jerry Jones, and Bill Knox.*

We were in the red light district, on its main street where all the brothels were. Joe was making sure I saw all the sights!

training. They all fly by the seat of their pants, following the rivers and mountains.

Bixby directed Sanford Kauffman to head to Alaska and work on the problem. The idea was to require the pilots to go out of Alaska periodically to update their skills. They would be trained in instrument flight and radio operations so they could rival any of the pilots in the Pan American system.

Kauffman went to Seattle to meet Joe Crosson and put the plan in motion. Crosson flew Kauffman to Fairbanks, where he toured the operations and was favorably impressed with the pilots.

Kauffman was welcomed at the Crosson home for a sumptuous meal and a hearty discussion of Alaska and the proposed changes in store for PAA. Joe and Lillian then gave him a ride to his hotel, with Joe at the wheel—a ride that Kauffman never forgot:

> It had been raining a lot and the roads were full of mud holes. He turned down a side street toward the hotel and I noticed his wife getting real mad. I didn't know what the problem was, but I soon found out, because we got stuck about halfway down the street— right in front of a whorehouse. We were in the red light district, on its main street where all the brothels were. Joe was making sure I saw all the sights!
>
> But we weren't there more than a minute when the door of a brothel opened and a woman who looked like the madam came out and walked over to the car. "What's the matter, Joe," she said. "Are you stalled? I'll get the girls out and we'll give you a push." And that's exactly what she proceeded to do. This bunch of shady ladies came running out, pushed on the car, and quickly had us rolling on our way.

Kauffman explained to the pilots in Fairbanks that instrument training would be necessary for them in order to maintain a regular schedule of flights in the multi-engine planes Pan American planned to buy for PAA. The Alaska pilots were skeptical of the need for

training: they already knew the rivers, forests, mountains, and valleys that guided them in poor weather. But Kauffman pressed his case, outlining the plan to send them and their families to Brownsville, Texas, for training; Pan Am would cover all expenses. The pilots warmed to the idea, and Crosson worked with Kauffman to develop a schedule for pilots to rotate to Texas.

With Crosson as part of the management team, Pacific Alaska Airways expanded operations to become the first modern airline in the Territory. PAA launched an ambitious plan to upgrade ground facilities throughout the system. A spacious new hangar built in Fairbanks included a machine shop for maintaining the newer aircraft.

Communications and weather-gathering remained a tremendous challenge. Over the next few years a series of radio stations was built, and eventually planes could be contacted anywhere along the routes. Stations were located about 250 miles apart and each employed a station operator. Often a married couple shared the responsibilities. Operators were trained in meteorology to accurately relay weather conditions to pilots and to other stations. By the end of 1939, PAA

▲ *Crew members load baggage and mail in wing compartments and the cabin of a new Lockheed Electra. Introduction of the twin-engine Lockheed Electra to Alaska in the mid-1930s was a giant step in modernizing flying in the north.*

2-16

▲ *Over the years,*
Fairbanks grew from the
little town Joe first saw in
1926 to this small city of
the late 1930s, with log
cabins giving way to
multistory buildings.

radio stations were operating at Fairbanks, Koyuk, Tanana, Nulato, Tanacross, Juneau, Ketchikan, McGrath, Flat, Bethel, and several locations in Canada.

Terminals were upgraded, routes extended, and new aircraft purchased. Crosson's days were kept busy between office duties and regular flying. He also made frequent business trips to the continental United States.

In September 1933, Crosson sweltered in Miami as he waited to pick up a new Consolidated Fleetster to bring back to Alaska. The big

single-engine plane could carry more passengers and freight than the
Fairchild 71, so PAA bought two of them to take over some of the
remote flying done by its fleet of Fairchilds.

After ferrying the plane to Alaska, Joe supervised the winterizing of
the new craft. In extreme cold temperatures, the blast of frigid air
through the cowling during flight kept radial engines from warming
up to their optimum operating temperature. The PAA crew built
shutters for the cowling so pilots could regulate operating
temperatures.

Skis presented another engineering challenge. In much of Alaska,
planes were of little value during the winter without skis. Most landing
strips were never plowed, and snow accumulated all winter long. Skis
also provided an additional measure of safety, because frozen rivers
and lakes and vast areas of snow-covered land could then be used as
emergency landing strips.

The two Fleetsters had a short career with PAA. During the spring
of 1934, the Russian ship *Chelyuskin* became frozen in the arctic ice off
Siberia and eventually sank, stranding more than one hundred people.
PAA agreed to sell the Fleetsters to the Soviet government for use in
the rescue. Two pilots from Russia arrived to pick up the craft. At that
time, Joe knew more about Siberian flying than any other pilot in the
world, because of his experiences during the search for Ben Eielson. But
offers by Joe and other arctic pilots to help in the rescue were refused.

The planes left Alaska with Russian pilots and two Alaskan
mechanics. Within days one plane was damaged beyond use. The
rescue was eventually accomplished after the survivors spent several
arduous weeks on the drifting ice.

A huge Ford single-engine freighter plane was brought in to
replace the Fleetsters. The plane was winterized at Fairbanks, and the
following summer it was outfitted with floats for water landings and
takeoffs. The plane, originally a Ford Tri-Motor, had been converted to
a more powerful single engine before being sent north. It could handle
large, bulky loads but was an unusual sight. On a huge set of floats it
made even a stranger picture.

A near disaster occurred as Joe tested the plane at Harding Lake.

*Joe knew more about
Siberian flying than any
other pilot in the world,
because of his
experiences during the
search for Ben Eielson.*

As Billy came around in
front of the moving
plane on one pass, his
outboard motor
sputtered and died,
and the wind pushed
the boat right at the
approaching plane.

The day was fairly windy, with a chop on the waves. As he slowly taxied into the wind, a boy in a small outboard-powered boat decided to take a closer look.

Billy O'Keefe headed his skiff out to the Ford and proceeded to circle the plane as it idled along. As Billy came around in front of the moving plane on one pass, his outboard motor sputtered and died, and the wind pushed the boat right at the approaching plane. Billy did the only thing he could and dove into the lake. Joe cut the power to the big radial engine, but it was too late. A sickening *thunk, thunk, thunk* filled the air as the big three-bladed prop shredded the skiff.

Although he was relieved that Billy wasn't hurt, Crosson's temper flared. The boy escaped with his life, but he couldn't avoid a tongue lashing from Crosson, usually an even-tempered person. Billy later told a friend: "I never knew Mr. Crosson could swear like that."

∽

WITH MORE AIR carriers competing for charter business in Alaska, it became apparent that PAA was in a position to make a unique contribution to the Territory. Pacific Alaska's strategy was to concentrate on scheduled passenger and mail service on a trunk system that connected the principal communities in the Territory and to expand into Southeast Alaska. With regular schedules established, the airline could then focus on linking Alaska more closely with the rest of the United States.

Joining the larger communities of Bethel, Anchorage, and Nome to the main hub in Fairbanks with scheduled flights was relatively easy. The flights were within a few hundred miles of Fairbanks, along familiar routes. The new radio stations made the schedule almost routine.

Expanding into Southeast Alaska was a different story. PAA wanted to link passengers from the population center in mainland Alaska to the steamship system and to the continental United States, and it needed to develop a route between Interior Alaska and Southeast Alaska. If successful, days of train and boat travel would be reduced to a four- or five-hour flight from Fairbanks to the capital city of Juneau.

◄ *Joe Crosson tested this huge, single-engine Ford plane on floats at Harding Lake in 1934. The test nearly ended in disaster when a local boy drove his motorboat directly in front of the plane.*

The challenges were daunting. Terrain was difficult, to say the least. Juneau is surrounded by immense jagged mountains that leap right out of the water, and pilots had not routinely crossed them. Distances were long, and few possibilities of safe emergency landing and takeoff existed within the vast coastal rain forests of Sitka spruce, cedars, and firs. Bad weather and pea-soup fog is legendary in Southeast, and no air navigation facilities existed.

Juneau had no runway; Pacific Alaska Airways would have to buy land and build an airport. A route had to be surveyed and chosen, emergency fields identified, and radio stations built.

In anticipation of the move into Southeast, PAA bought a small airline already operating in the region. The purchase of Alaska Southern Airways gave PAA miscellaneous ground equipment and facilities at Juneau, Ketchikan, and Seattle, and three more aircraft: a Fairchild 71, a Lockheed Vega, and a Loening Amphibian.

During 1933 and 1934 a great deal of effort was focused on the Fairbanks-to-Juneau route. Crosson made a series of survey flights between the two cities. The route eventually chosen aimed north from Juneau across the coastal mountains to Whitehorse in Canada's Yukon

PAA "Electra" at Juneau Airport
@36 ORDWAY. 35446

▲ *Alaskan peaks and the Mendenhall Glacier look down on a sleek ten-passenger Lockheed Electra at the Juneau airport. Pacific Alaska Airways built the runway in the mid-1930s to allow dependable air service to Alaska's capital, where previously only floatplanes could land.*

Territory, then northwest to Fairbanks. An emergency field was built at Burwash Landing in Yukon Territory, the strip at Tanacross, Alaska, was improved for emergency landings, and the runway at Whitehorse was lengthened and improved.

The most daunting task was at Juneau. Although it was the capital city of the Territory, Juneau had no runway. The town is nestled between the mountains on Gastineau Channel, part of the waterway that connects the Inside Passage to the Pacific Ocean. The channel is ice-free year-round, and all flights in and out of Juneau were by floatplane.

The need for floats at Juneau was a significant problem for planes traveling from the Alaska mainland, where skis were a necessity during the winter. Flights that took off on skis from Fairbanks had to land on frozen lakes near Juneau so that the skis could be removed and replaced with floats. Pilots then faced a tricky takeoff from the ice on floats before they could head for the capital. An equally tricky float landing on ice awaited the pilots when they returned from Juneau to the frozen lake, where mechanics would switch the floats back to skis.

Crosson made a practice of noting possible landing spots and sharing this information with the other pilots.

Pacific Alaska Airways chose Don Abel to take on the challenge of building a Juneau runway. Abel had supervised construction of both the new hangar at Fairbanks and the emergency landing strip at Burwash Landing.

Progress on the runway was swift, and the work ran ahead of schedule. When the runway was completed, pilots could fly from the Interior to Alaska's capital and land on wheels for the first time. Scheduled air service between Juneau and Fairbanks was officially started April 1, 1935. A sleek new Lockheed Electra 10B was chosen for the historic flight that opened a new era in Alaska aviation.

New airplane or old, Crosson was always conscious of the dangers facing PAA pilots on every cross-country flight. Trips often included hundreds of miles over rugged territory offering little chance for emergency landing. Crosson made a practice of noting possible landing spots and sharing this information with the other pilots. On one trip to Juneau he spotted a stretch of beach that might serve as an emergency strip.

Radioman Bob Gleason remembered that flight: "We were flying over Berners Bay on Lynn Canal headed into Juneau. The beach was gravel and Joe thought it would hold the Electra." After looking it over, Crosson set up an approach between towering forest and cold saltwater and brought the Lockheed down on the beach. According to Gleason, "It was a big chance, but he knew the pilots needed an option if the weather went down." After the landing, Joe simply fed in the power and the plane bounced along the rough gravel and climbed back into the air. The new information was passed on to the PAA pilots.

$\sim$

RADIO OPERATOR Bob Gleason handed Joe Crosson a message—an unusual one for Fairbanks. On this day in July 1938, a crew of

Concerned about having to ditch in the ocean, Hughes had filled all open space in the cabin and wings with Ping-Pong balls. According to his calculations, the little balls would keep the ship from sinking.

round-the-world fliers were requesting that all available police be on hand to cordon off the area where their Lockheed Electra would park. In addition, no one but Pacific Alaska Airways personnel would be allowed to approach the plane.

Crosson looked curiously at the message. He knew the people in Fairbanks would be on hand in great numbers to meet the world fliers, but extreme measures would not be necessary. No one would harm the plane. But the pilot's wishes would be honored. (Years later the odd request in Fairbanks would be looked on as normal for the increasingly eccentric pilot.)

The crowd cheered as the big twin-engine plane emerged from a layer of broken clouds. The dirt runway at Weeks Field had been lengthened for the occasion. Crosson marked down the official moment the Lockheed's tires touched ground. It was 2:17 P.M., the time recorded by the National Aeronautical Association, the organization in charge of monitoring attempts at new flight records.

As the props stopped turning, the rear hatch on the sleek silver cabin opened and the tired occupants emerged. Four crew members and the tall pilot, Texas millionaire Howard Hughes, were out to break Wiley Post's record time for an around-the-world flight. The touchdown in Fairbanks all but ensured they would.

One of the guests greeting Hughes was Mae Post, Wiley's widow. Mae was in Alaska staying with the Crossons and learning firsthand what Wiley had loved about the Territory.

Crosson directed the mechanics as they went about their business servicing the big radial engines and pumping on seventeen hundred gallons of av gas. In little more than an hour the plane was ready to continue.

During the servicing, mechanics emptied the plane of an unusual cargo, much to the delight of local kids. Concerned about having to ditch in the ocean, Hughes had filled all open space in the cabin and wings with Ping-Pong balls. According to his calculations, the little balls would keep the ship from sinking.

The flight from Fairbanks through Canada and on to New York was over land, and this flotation was no longer needed. So out came hundreds and hundreds of Ping-Pong balls. When Hughes took off and pointed the Lockheed to the southeast at 3:35 in the afternoon, eager children scooped up the little white treasures.

Howard Hughes appreciated Crosson's help in his world-record quest, and years later he returned a favor to Lillian. In the 1960s Lillian was on a familiarization tour in Las Vegas for her travel agency. She visited a Hughes-owned hotel and offered her business card to a clerk who recognized the name and struck up a conversation. During their talk Lillian mentioned that she had decided to splurge and see the most popular dinner show in town, but that it was sold out. The clerk encouraged her to go to the show anyway and see if any seats were open. Lillian took his advice, and when she showed up, the headwaiter escorted her to a front row table, where she was served a wonderful dinner and enjoyed the best seat in the house. When she went to pay the bill, she was told it had been covered by Howard Hughes.

In 1938, PAA was making dramatic advances in Alaskan aviation, but the success had little effect on Crosson's demeanor. He always showed extreme consideration for his passengers. For instance, he knew that others in the plane became uneasy when flying through the narrow Taku Pass. He realized that travelers could see only the sheer rock walls of the canyon through their side windows. So when he was at the controls, Crosson always opened the cockpit door to share the pilot's view, which allowed passengers to see that their course through the pass was open.

No matter what title he held or what plane he flew, Crosson remained an easygoing bush pilot. One young pilot, Bill Lavery, later recalled a flight with Crosson from Fairbanks:

> Joe Crosson—he was the most calm pilot that I've ever been with. . . . We were going from here to Whitehorse, in the Lockheed and, oh boy we got iced up and he said, "You ever flown one when it was all iced up?" I said nope, he said, "Grab a hold and just be careful, don't let the wings get down on you or anything, don't let it slow up or you'll stall out." And he sat there and started buffing his fingernails. I'll never forget that as long as I live.

"You ever flown one when it was all iced up?" I said nope, he said, "Grab a hold and just be careful, don't let the wings get down on you or anything, don't let it slow up or you'll stall out."

Inaugural flight of the Sikorsky S-42 seaplane

21

ALASKA TO SEATTLE

1938-1940. The final link in the Pacific Alaska Airways system was Seattle. PAA, with Crosson at the helm, had secured mail contracts between Juneau and Fairbanks and on much of the trunk route system within the Territory. A connection to Seattle would provide a route so passengers as well as mail could reach Alaska in hours by air instead of in days by sea.

Plans called for expansion of land facilities and purchase of four-engine land planes to establish an all-American route from Seattle to Juneau. But when it became apparent that the four-engine Boeing 307 passenger liners that Pacific Alaska intended to use would not be available for several years, the use of seaplanes was considered.

During the end of 1938 and the beginning of 1939, Pacific Alaska embarked on a series of flights to explore connecting Seattle, Ketchikan, and Juneau. The twin-engine Sikorsky S-43 amphibian, similar to flying boats used in the Pan American system in South America, was designed to land on water but could also land on runways with gear extended, and this plane was chosen for the job. Flights were given provisional authorization by the Civil Aeronautics Authority and PAA was allowed to carry mail but not passengers.

Before the Sikorskys could fly the route, there was a lot of work to

May 13, 1940

Igor Sikorsky makes the first free flight in his VS-300 helicopter at Stratford, Connecticut.

◄ *Territorial Governor Ernest Gruening (second from left) welcomes the inaugural flight of the Sikorsky S-42 seaplane, the Pan Am Clipper, from Seattle to Juneau on June 20, 1940. With the governor are the plane's captain Robbie Robbins (left), Joe Crosson, and first officer Jerry Jones.*

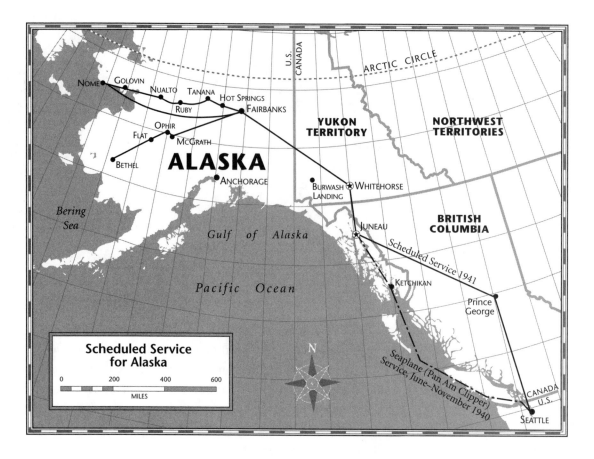

do. Even though the S-43s could land on runways, Pan Am decided to
establish sea bases in all three cities of the route—Seattle, Ketchikan,
and Juneau. At each location, waterfront sites and operations and
administration buildings were leased or constructed. Marine barges,
docks, patrol and service launches, terminals, and communication
facilities were set up at all three places. Sheltered waters for safe landings,
and alternate landing areas in case of bad weather, were located. Amid
fanfare by Pacific Alaska, the first flights began in August 1938.

A crowd of excited well-wishers watched late in the afternoon of
August 7 as the Sikorsky, one of the largest craft ever to arrive at
Juneau, touched down at the PAA airfield outside the city, arriving
from Seattle, via Ketchikan. Regular service to the continental United
States was now one step closer.

A total of eighteen Sikorsky flights carrying mail, freight, and PAA personnel were made by the end of January 1939. Much was learned, but overall the lessons were disappointing. The route traversed American territory and American or international waters, and traveled up the forested coast from Seattle to the Inside Passage. However, dangerous flying conditions in the often cloudy and rainy passage required the plane to fly out over the open ocean for much of the route, a risky maneuver for the S-43. If one of the two engines faltered, the plane could fly for only a limited time before being forced to land in the ocean. Pan Am decided to stop the flights and consider alternative equipment and routes. The three bases were closed, employees reassigned, and equipment absorbed into the Pan American system.

Despite Crosson's dedication to connecting Alaska to the continental states with scheduled service, the subject hung in limbo for eighteen months. Lockheed Electras were used on the route on a charter basis and no schedule was established. Crosson was unsuccessful in obtaining either long-range, twin-engine flying boats or the four-engine land planes originally requested for flights to Alaska. Finally a decision was announced to reestablish the route, this time using four-engine flying boats—the Sikorsky S-42 seaplanes that were known as Pan Am Clippers.

The seaplanes were proven in the Pan American fleet. They were efficient and had a record of trouble-free operation. Unlike the S-43,

▲ Arrival of the Sikorsky S-43 flying boat in Ketchikan on August 7, 1938, marked the first serious attempt to begin providing scheduled service between Alaska and the forty-eight states.

▲ Operating flying boats like this Sikorsky S-42 in Alaska offered many new challenges to Pacific Alaska Airways. Water-based operations required the company to acquire barges and boats to tend the aircraft, such as this fuel barge at Ketchikan.

they could not also land on wheels, but the strong hull would allow safe landings in the open ocean if an emergency ever forced the pilots to make that decision. They dwarfed the S-43s. With four dependable Pratt & Whitney Hornet radials, the big seaplanes could carry thirty-two passengers in comfort over the long trip from Seattle to Juneau.

Because the seaplane bases used in the S-43 flights in 1938 had been disassembled, new bases were established to accommodate the larger four-engine craft. At Lake Washington in Seattle, an administration and communications building was built, along with a mooring dock. At rainy Ketchikan, no mooring space was available along the docks, so a barge was fitted with a refueling facility and mooring gear. A launch was acquired to move passengers and cargo to and from shore. At Juneau, suitable moorage was miles away from downtown. New administration and passenger facilities were built, and mooring and refueling equipment put in place.

On June 20, 1940, the Alaska Clipper lifted off the placid waters of Lake Washington on the inaugural flight. Pacific Alaska Airways made sure the news traveled across the country by inviting reporters, along with congressmen, representatives of the Civil Aeronautics Authority, politically powerful agency heads, and businessmen, on the historic flight. Joe Crosson had worked toward this goal for years and had been strongly encouraged by New York headquarters to sit in the left seat as pilot-in-command. But Crosson thought that assigning himself as pilot would be stepping on the toes of his staff, and he wouldn't do it.

Instead he assigned two of the Alaskan pilots he had known and respected for years to the controls.

Robbie Robbins and Jerry Jones piloted the first flight of the Alaska Clipper, carrying twenty-six passengers, among them Joe Crosson. Crowds gathered at the Auk Bay facility outside of Juneau to welcome the shiny silver flying boat, but the crew radioed that thick fog about fifteen miles out of town forced a change in plans. Robbins set the Clipper down on Gastineau Channel and taxied the last few miles into Juneau. The crowd had enough time to drive back to town and greet the passengers as they disembarked. Governor Ernest Gruening welcomed the passengers to Juneau and hosted them at a reception and dinner.

The following day, Crosson flew an Electra to his old hometown of Fairbanks to deliver the load of airmail that had come up from Seattle aboard the Alaska Clipper. The other passengers reboarded the Clipper for the flight back to Seattle. The flying boat also carried Governor Gruening and 720 pounds of airmail. One other interesting piece of cargo was aboard: a seven-foot-tall totem pole carved for President Franklin Delano Roosevelt by students at Wrangell Institute.

Establishing service between the forty-eight states and Alaska was the most important step taken since Pacific Alaska Airways was first formed. Thousands of hours in the sky during the past decade and a half had taken Joe Crosson from the frigid open-cockpits of planes flying over Interior Alaska to the shores of Lake Washington in Seattle to establish a seaplane base. By 1940, most of his work was supervising a huge effort in Washington state, so Joe, Lillian, and their sons moved to Seattle.

Thousands of hours in the sky during the past decade and a half had taken Joe Crosson from the frigid open-cockpits of planes flying over Interior Alaska to the shores of Lake Washington in Seattle to establish a seaplane base

~

THE SEAPLANE BASE at Sand Point on Lake Washington was convenient for the Crossons, just a few miles from their new home at Sheridan Beach. Although busy at his bustling office at the White Henry Stewart Building in downtown Seattle, Crosson was equally at home with the crew at Sand Point. Wandering through the hangar, he greeted each of the employees, genuinely interested in what they had to say. If another

Passengers and mail traveled between Seattle's Boeing Field and Fairbanks in one day, with stops in Prince George, Juneau, and Whitehorse.

hand was needed, Crosson would roll up his own sleeves and pitch in. As one young member of the Sand Point crew, Burt Armstrong, put it, "Joe was one of the nicest guys in the world. You never felt like you worked for him, you worked with him."

Despite meticulous planning and promotion of the new route to Alaska, troubles began to arise during the cooling days of autumn. Cold, wet weather in Southeast Alaska brought difficulties to the flying boat operation. No suitable method of preheating the large plane's engines had been devised, and low temperatures made them difficult to start. Passengers were delayed, and schedules became impossible to keep. The dependability that PAA and Pan Am took pride in maintaining was threatened. In November the flights were discontinued, and once again the seaplane facilities were closed. It now appeared clear that any permanent route to Alaska could not rely on seaplanes.

Crosson ordered survey flights in a DC-3 to find a suitable land route between Seattle and Alaska. The long trip would necessitate a refueling stop, and Prince George, British Columbia, was the logical place. An operations building and refueling equipment were put in place at Prince George. In addition, a radio station and navigation beacon were placed there and at Dease Lake and Takla Landing. When everything was in order, the route from Seattle to Alaska was again established, this time over land.

In March 1941, the first scheduled overland flights commenced in twin-engine Lockheed Electras. Passengers and mail traveled between Seattle's Boeing Field and Fairbanks in one day, with stops in Prince George, Juneau, and Whitehorse. Within two months, sleek new twin-engine Lockheed Lodestars, capable of hauling heavier cargo loads over longer distances, were making the flights to Alaska, while the Electras handled most of the trunk routes within the Territory. It had been sixteen years since Joe took his first flight in the north, and he remained a central figure all that time in the development of Alaskan aviation.

Aviation was also growing rapidly in the Seattle area, where the Crosson family was now living. The expansion of Pacific Alaska Airways to Seattle coincided with a burgeoning of aviation in the Pacific Northwest. Boeing was building more and larger airplanes, and

◄ Lockheed Lodestars like the one flying here soon replaced the Lockheed Electras that established land-based scheduled service to Alaska from Seattle in March 1941. With stops in British Columbia and the Yukon, Pacific Alaska Airways was able to provide uninterrupted scheduled service between Alaska and the continental United States.

scheduled commercial flights were putting a strain on Boeing Field. Crosson was one of the experts chosen by the Civil Aeronautics Authority to recommend a location for a larger international airport.

Crosson flew regularly for months in a Lockheed Electra in all kinds of weather, looking over the area. He discovered that Paine Field, north of Seattle, was often fog-free when the city and Boeing Field were socked in. Pan American built a new hangar at Payne Field in anticipation of the new airport.

Politics entered the decision, and although Crosson's observations were valid, the CAA settled on an area south of Seattle, between Seattle and Tacoma, for the new airport. The Army Air Corps was quick to capitalize on Joe's recommendation, took over the Paine Field property, and established the Paine Field Army Air Corps Base.

In May 1941, Pan American decided that Pacific Alaska Airways should become a stand-alone division of Pan Am. Some in the corporate offices had argued that instead, PAA should be absorbed by Pan Am's Pacific Division, which operated out of Oakland, California. But Vice President Harold Bixby had watched Crosson guide the operation from an unscheduled charter business with a band of bush pilots in a mixed fleet of airplanes to a highly organized scheduled airline that had expanded successfully to the mainland. According to Bob Gleason, "Bixby supported Joe and PAA. He said, 'These guys started this thing in Alaska and they worked their way down to Seattle. Now it should remain a division, and they should run it.'"

Pacific Alaska Airways became the Alaska Division, and at thirty-seven years old, Joe Crosson was named division manager, the youngest ever in the history of Pan American Airways.

The analyst group, with Joe on left

22

THE WAR YEARS

Seattle, 1940-1944. The world was now focusing on a war that was spreading from Germany and Japan around the globe. U.S. military planners needed to be prepared to protect America from potential enemies, and they realized Alaska was a key piece of the world puzzle. But if it became necessary to fight in northern climates, American military men were not prepared. As the Department of Defense sought information about flying and fighting in the north, Joe Crosson became involved.

When Crosson was general manager of Pacific Alaska Airways in the late 1930s, the company provided the U.S. military with hard-earned knowledge gathered by pilots and mechanics during their decades of work in the Arctic. PAA's experience in developing wing covers, skis, engine preheating, radio communications, and navigation aids gave the military valuable insight into flying in the north. PAA also offered to let the military use its facilities in Alaska. By the time the United States entered the war, a secret contract had been signed giving the Navy access to all Pacific Alaska Airways ground and communication facilities and to its personnel. Crosson's expertise was highly valued by the Navy.

The Army Air Corps hired polar explorer Vilhjalmur Stefansson to

August 8, 1940

Production of airplanes in the United States reaches 900 per month.

◄ *Territorial Governor Ernest Gruening (in dark leather coat with white trim) meets with members of the Army's operations analyst group in the Aleutian Islands during 1943. Joe Crosson, a member of the analyst group, is at far left.*

*The expected commission
didn't materialize and,
meanwhile, at the age of
thirty-seven, Joe began
experiencing health
problems for the first time
in his life.*

write an arctic survival manual, and Stefansson turned to Crosson for information based on his survival experiences. Joe and Lillian visited Stefansson in New York several times, and Lillian remembers elegant dinners at the explorer's home while they discussed flying in the Arctic.

General Hap Arnold, an Army Air Corps visionary, recognized the importance of Alaska to U.S. security. Crosson and Arnold had been friends since 1934, when Arnold led a flight of Army Air Corps bombers to Alaska to conduct an aerial survey of the Territory. Pacific Alaska Airways had made its operations available to the Army during that tour, and Crosson had been a great help to the crews.

In 1940, Arnold toured Alaska again, this time to check out aviation facilities. Crosson met the general in Juneau to look over PAA's runway and determine whether it was suitable as a secondary field for the military. Arnold's DC-3 had no trouble landing or taking off, and both men agreed the field could handle military aircraft.

As the war heated up, Crosson wanted to enter the fray in uniform. Arnold wrote to Crosson, stating that he had "issued instructions" to have him commissioned as a major in the Air Corps Reserve.

The expected commission didn't materialize and, meanwhile, at the age of thirty-seven, Joe began experiencing health problems for the first time in his life. Shortly after the Crosson family moved to Seattle in 1940, he endured an attack of severe abdominal pain. Over the next year and a half he suffered from a combination of aching joints, headaches, and intestinal pains. His doctors ruled out problems with gall bladder or kidneys, but no firm diagnosis was made and Joe continued to work.

The malady intensified in April 1942, when Crosson suffered severe headaches and pain in his neck. His doctor treated him for sinus problems and prescribed sulfathiazole, a sulfa drug used as an early antibiotic. He was also advised to go into the hospital, but instead chose to stick to his regular schedule.

Within a day, Crosson's face and hands became swollen, with large, itchy blotches. His blood pressure, which had been noted as "a bit high" the previous February, began to rise. The following afternoon while working in his office, he suddenly noticed a blur in the vision of his right eye. His increasing blood pressure had caused one of the arteries in his eye to burst. He finally consented to enter the hospital.

Crosson was critically ill as his blood pressure continued to climb to dangerous levels. "He almost died that night," Lillian remembered. Tests revealed problems with his kidneys, his body was racked with pain, and his vision became worse as several smaller arteries in his eyes burst. Doctors could find nothing to help except painkillers.

Finally, after two weeks, Crosson's vision began to improve, the pain subsided, and his blood pressure began to drop. After a month in the hospital, he was allowed to return home. He had lost more than twenty pounds, but his spirit remained strong and he was determined to recover.

Crosson's younger sister Zelma, a registered nurse, came to help during his recuperation in Seattle. But after Joe had been home for only a few days, Zelma and the three sons of Joe and Lillian—Joe Jr., Don, and Bob—contracted strep throat. All four were given sulfathiazole to fight the infection—the same drug given earlier to Joe.

Don recovered quickly. However, Zelma's face became swollen and blotched with spots. Joe Jr. suffered a similar reaction, but four-year-old Bob had the worst of it. He had to be hospitalized for several blood transfusions.

It turned out that for Zelma and two of the three young boys, the cure was perhaps worse than the disease. They had suffered severe allergic reactions to sulfathiazole. Joe's medical conditions were complicated by his allergy to this sulfa drug that had been given to him to help combat his symptoms.

Crosson was not at full strength and couldn't concentrate on work during the next few months. He occasionally went to the office, but recuperation was slow. For several months he relied on his old friend and colleague, radioman Bob Gleason, to act for him during periods when his illness kept him off the job.

In one of the toughest consequences of his illness, Crosson failed a medical exam in 1942 and his pilot's license was put on hold. His blood pressure had dropped from critical levels, but it remained high enough to prevent him from passing a flight physical again until 1946.

"He almost died that night," Lillian remembered. Tests revealed problems with his kidneys, his body was racked with pain, and his vision became worse as several smaller arteries in his eyes burst.

*He was still a civilian—
but he was now
serving two branches
of the armed services,
each of which coveted
his assistance.*

Later in 1942, high blood pressure also put an end to another attempt by Crosson and Hap Arnold to have Joe commissioned in the reserves. By December 1942, Joe was at the helm of Pan American's new Alaska Division, and frequent trips to New York were worked into his schedule.

~

IN MARCH 1943, Hap Arnold found a way to tap Crosson's knowledge for the war effort even if he couldn't turn Joe into a military officer. Arnold recommended Crosson for temporary but full-time service with a group of civilians who were charged with analyzing military operations in the Aleutian Islands.

The islands had been a focus of military activity before the war, and this only intensified following Japanese bombing at Dutch Harbor in the Aleutians in June 1942. The Eleventh Air Force of the Army Air Corps was operating in the region, and losses of aircraft and lives due to flying conditions in the north were mounting. Arnold hoped Crosson could make recommendations to improve the situation.

Pan American Vice President Harold Bixby received a confidential letter from the Army's assistant chief of staff, Brigadier General R. G. Moses, on March 31, 1943, requesting Joe's service for the Aleutians operations analyst group. The letter said Joe's qualifications made him "nearly indispensable."

Days later Bixby received another confidential document, this time from the Office of the U.S. Navy, arguing that Crosson should not be fully released to serve with the operations analyst group because he was so vital to the Navy's contracted work with Pan American.

Bixby agreed that Joe should serve as an operations analyst. A few months before, Crosson had been frustrated by not being accepted to serve his country in uniform. He was still a civilian—but he was now serving two branches of the armed services, each of which coveted his assistance.

The operations analyst group included radio and radar experts from outside Alaska, in addition to Crosson and his old friend, weather forecaster Howard J. Thompson from Anchorage. Joe's responsibility was to make recommendations of how to improve flying techniques.

The group toured the Aleutians theater of operations in May and June of 1943. The Army's history of the analyst group singled out Thompson and Crosson and gives insight into their contributions:

> In short order, Crosson and Thompson made surveys of conditions in their specialized fields, pointing out deficiencies in the military set-up and suggesting in detail improved procedures in the light of civilian experience with local conditions. By the time these men left in July 1943, programs for improving operations along the lines they had recommended were already underway.

Joe continued to try to enter the military in uniform. In August 1943 a movement to commission him as an officer in the Navy surfaced, with no more luck than previous efforts. He had still not fully regained his health.

In October 1943, the War Department asked Crosson to conduct an operations analysis of the Burma-India theater of operations, which was in the process of building up bases for B-29s flying between Burma and Japan. Although flattered by the request, Joe had to decline. Pan American believed Joe's expertise was arctic flying and would not support the request for him to travel to Asia.

A final effort by General Hap Arnold, as commanding general of the Army Air Force, was made to "draft" Joe. An October 13, 1943, telegram directed his subordinates to request that Pan American Airways release Crosson from duty so he could be commissioned, this time as a lieutenant colonel. But as before, the commission did not materialize.

Although he was frustrated and may have felt he failed in his efforts to help in the war effort, Crosson made a great contribution to the military and to his country. It was not what he had originally envisioned—in uniform, possibly at the controls of a plane—but Joe

It was not what he had originally envisioned—in uniform, possibly at the controls of a plane—but Joe did help the United States win the war.

A variety of isolated incidents solidified in his mind and convinced him to change his path.

did help the United States win the war. His knowledge of flying in the north and his recommendations saved American lives.

~

FOLLOWING HIS ASSIGNMENT in the Aleutians, Crosson resumed duties with the Alaska Division of Pan American. He contemplated how things had changed. During his time with the company, he had risen from chief pilot for Pacific Alaska Airways to a division manager in the Pan American system. Under Joe's supervision, the number of employees at Pacific Alaska Airways and then the Alaska Division had increased from thirty-nine to more than three hundred, and thousands of passengers were now traveling each year on Pan Am's Alaska routes.

Throughout his career with Pan Am, Joe had focused on the Territory. His decisions were based on what was good for Alaska. Like all profitable companies, Pan American focused on what was good for Pan American. Too many times the difference in philosophy and resulting decisions from faraway in New York made Joe uncomfortable, and his discomfort had grown over the years. A variety of isolated incidents solidified in his mind and convinced him to change his path.

The company's focus on publicity often left Joe, who did not relish the limelight, in conflict. The publicity stunt that delayed his flight when he was returning the bodies of Wiley Post and Will Rogers still pained him. Refusals from New York to requests for better equipment for the Alaska Division were harder to accept with each passing year. And now, despite his many contributions to aviation over the years, his health problems prevented him from passing a flight physical. Even though he remained division manager, Pan American no longer considered him a pilot.

Crosson knew it was time to leave, and in early 1944, he resigned from Pan Am. Northwest Airlines immediately tried to hire him, but he did not want to work for another large corporation. He needed a change, and plotted a new course for his career. For the first time since his barnstorming days in San Diego, he went to work for himself.

Joe and "Tex" Rankin

23

AVIATION ENTREPRENEUR

Seattle, 1944-1949. Joe Crosson's career in aviation took a huge turn following his resignation from Pan Am. Along with several partners, he bought Northwest Air Service, a successful parts and maintenance operation with a hangar and repair shop at Boeing Field in Seattle.

Joining him in the venture were fellow bush pilot Noel Wien, who was also now living in Seattle; John Healy, a businessman and former neighbor of Crosson's; and Charlie Babb, a broker of used aircraft and surplus parts. Their plan was to supply airplanes, parts, and mechanical services to companies flying in Alaska and the Northwest, with Joe as general manager.

Life at Northwest Air Service was a far cry from the corporate days at Pan Am. It was the perfect business for Joe, who knew people from one end of Alaska to the other. He could visit with Alaska pilots coming and going at Boeing Field on their travels from the Territory, and he could meet with his colleagues who came to the Boeing airplane factory.

By the end of World War II, Northwest Air Service had secured all of the overhaul and repair business for Alaska Coastal Airways, based in Juneau. The outfit operated a small fleet of seaplanes that linked Alaska's coastal communities with Seattle. Crosson's operation handled

October 14, 1947

U.S. Army Air Corps pilot Chuck Yeager becomes the first person to break the sound barrier, flying the X-1 at Mach 1.07 (650 miles per hour) at 42,000 feet altitude.

◄ *Joe Crosson (left) and manufacturer "Tex" Rankin pose with a new Seabee at the aircraft factory in New York. Joe saw the little amphibian as an answer to operations in remote areas of Alaska.*

"He starts letting down through the soup and came out right over the end of the runway. That guy had the instincts of a bird."

overhaul of the Pratt & Whitney radial engines and airframe work. In addition, Bob Ellis, the owner of another Southeast Alaska air carrier, shipped engines from his planes in Ketchikan down to Northwest Air Service for work.

Burt Armstrong, who had worked for Pan Am on its Sand Point crew, welcomed the chance to join Crosson at Northwest Air Service. Armstrong said it was never possible to guess who might visit Crosson at the hangar. An old prospector from Alaska might show up, looking for a grubstake, followed by Jackie Cochran, one of the most famous lady race pilots in history. Young military pilots on their way to Alaska regularly stopped by for information about flying in the Arctic. Bob Reeve of Reeve Aleutian Airways might visit, followed by an old mechanic friend, and then by retired General Jimmy Doolittle.

Armstrong found the same thing when he traveled with Crosson on buying trips: "Joe knew people all over the world. No matter where we went, Joe knew somebody." But despite the celebrity of his employer, Armstrong was impressed that Joe remained modest. "I never saw him try to get in the limelight. He didn't want to. He was just the opposite of most of the glory hounds."

Before Crosson's health improved enough to pass his flight physical during late 1946, Armstrong was called upon to be the official pilot when Crosson flew somewhere. Armstrong explained how it worked: "He'd say, 'Burt, you gotta take me to . . . ,' but on those trips I was just the license. Joe handled the controls and I was just along for the ride."

Armstrong especially remembered a short flight from Seattle to Bremerton, Crosson at the controls as usual. Radio navigation aids were becoming more common, but the Stinson they flew did not carry any of the new equipment. With the little plane chugging above a never-ending sea of thick clouds, Armstrong became worried about finding the Bremerton airport. Crosson seemed unconcerned. After a while Crosson said, "The airport's right there." Armstrong couldn't see a thing.

"He starts letting down through the soup," Armstrong said, "and came out right over the end of the runway. That guy had the instincts of a bird."

Northwest Air Service became a dealer for Seabee light airplanes, which could operate both on land and water. The sturdy little amphibians were made in New York by Republic Aviation, which had built SBD dive bombers during World War II. Crosson fell in love with the ungainly looking little Seabee. While many thought the craft was underpowered, Crosson found it to be easy flying and versatile, perfect for small operations in Alaska. The Seabee carried four passengers and had wheels that could be lowered when the pilot operated a small hydraulic hand pump. To show how strong the hull was built, engineers landed one of the prototypes on the tarmac without lowering the wheels.

Crosson flew out to the Seabee factory to pick up one of the first craft off the assembly line and fly it to the Northwest. Back above Seattle, Crosson buzzed Sheridan Beach on Lake Washington, where he knew his sons would be swimming, and landed outside the swimming area. "We swam out to the plane and looked it over," son Don recalls. "Dad opened the hatch and talked to us. . . "

The Seabee became Crosson's commuter vehicle. On most mornings, he drove the short distance from his home to Kenmore Air at the end of Lake Washington, flew in a Seabee to his job at Northwest Air Service, and in the evening commuted home in the little plane.

Crosson's son Bob recalls that other kids back then were in awe of pilots and flying, but air travel was the norm in his family. In the Crosson household, it was completely natural to climb into an airplane for travel. "I thought everyone's dad flew to work in the morning," Bob said.

At least one of Crosson's flights in a Seabee was far from routine. He found himself over Lake Washington with the landing gear dangling. A broken weld prevented him from either raising the dangling wheels to allow a water landing or locking them down for a runway landing.

The Seabee manufacturer had told him what to do in such a predicament. He had even practiced the maneuver: flying inches above the water and allowing the dangling wheels to touch the surface and be kicked back into place. Now he repeatedly tried the technique, but it didn't work. The wheels were still loose.

In the Crosson household, it was completely natural to climb into an airplane for travel. "I thought everyone's dad flew to work in the morning," Bob said.

Crosson touched down on the water just as the plane stalled. A sheet of spray erupted as the gear dug into the waves and the Seabee settled on the lake.

Crosson now decided to land on the water, another dangerous proposition. If the plane was going too fast when it landed, it would cartwheel as the dangling gear hit the water. But if the plane was going too slow, it would stall before touching down and spin into the water. The only way the landing would work was if the craft stalled just as the wheel touched the water. In that way the Seabee would be too low to spin, and moving too slowly to cartwheel.

As if it was something he did daily, Crosson touched down on the water just as the plane stalled. A sheet of spray erupted as the gear dug into the waves and the Seabee settled on the lake. Crosson simply taxied to the beach, and Kenmore Air mechanics repaired the broken weld.

Another adventure in a Seabee was less dangerous and more rewarding. Crosson loved to prowl the junkyards and surplus-equipment yards looking for aircraft parts that he could use at Northwest. On one trip, Burt Armstrong spotted a case of surplus sea markers, containers of dye used by the Navy to mark locations in the water. The cans were selling for a nickel each, and Joe bought the lot—about five dollars worth.

"Wouldn't these be good for marking schools of fish?" Armstrong asked. With the markers in hand, Crosson and Armstrong flew a Seabee down to Pacific Beach, Washington, to demonstrate the plane to operators of a fleet of tuna boats.

Crosson offered to fly the Seabee over schools of tuna and drop the markers for one dollar a can. The tuna captains agreed. After a few drops of the cans proved successful, the fleet owner not only purchased the rest of the markers for a dollar a can, but he also bought the Seabee to go with them.

Crosson took great pride in his skills as an aircraft mechanic, and he also put this talent to use on the family car. During World War II, he organized a driving trip with his family to Montana. The family would enjoy a vacation, and Crosson planned to purchase some used airplanes. Gasoline was being rationed, and the poor quality of the fuel meant poor performance, especially at high altitudes. Before the trip, Crosson went to work on the family's 1941 Chrysler, adding a fuel-injection

system similar to that used on fighter planes. The drive over the 8,800-foot mountain pass on the way to Montana was effortless.

~

ON MAY 4, 1946, Lillian delivered their fourth child and first daughter, Susan. Joe delighted in showing her off and spent hours with "Susie Q" in a rocking chair at night, helping her fall asleep. Joe's parents Esler and Elizabeth now lived in a small house behind the main Crosson home. During the war Esler cultivated a large garden and enough chickens to

▲ *Remote lodges throughout Alaska and the Northwest were natural customers for the Seabee. Joe, as a dealer for the airplane, often demonstrated the versatile qualities of the amphibian, shown here in British Columbia.*

▲ *Joe and Lillian and*
their daughter Sue took
an outing to the San Juan
Islands of Washington
state in a Seabee, in the
spring of 1949.

keep the whole neighborhood in fresh vegetables and eggs. He delighted the local kids with a pet pig on a leash that carried his newspaper.

When the Crosson family moved from Alaska to Seattle, the little silver car Joe had built for the boys came along. Joe replaced the motor with a more powerful two-cylinder model and even added an automatic transmission. The house in Lake Forest Park had a circular driveway, which became the new racetrack. By this time, young Bob was the smallest driver, just able to peek over the steering wheel, and it was Don's turn to pull his younger brother out of the hedge after a wrong turn. As in Fairbanks, the little race car helped make the Crosson house the most popular one in the neighborhood.

Joe Jr. was a good athlete, and the family cheered him on at track meets and football games. When the boys joined Boy Scouts, Joe took a turn as Scout leader. He helped the boys construct frames for backpacks, and he hiked and camped in the Olympic and Cascade Mountains with the Scouts. On one occasion he flew Joe Jr.'s Scout patrol across Hood Canal for a campout. It was possibly the adventure of a lifetime for many of the boys, but it was just another trip for Joe Jr. "Aviation was always there," he said. "At the time, I guess I took it for granted."

Crosson shared his love for flying with his sons. Don worked for his dad at Boeing Field, cleaning surplus parts for a dollar a day. The pay wasn't nearly as good as the fringe benefits. On lucky afternoons Joe took Don flying, in whatever plane he had at the field that day. One afternoon he took Don up for a ride in a big single-engine SBD dive bomber. Don was thrilled when his dad let him take the controls of the bomber and coached him through some maneuvers.

In late June 1947, Joe took his eldest son on a flight to Alaska to deliver the first of many Seabees sold in the Territory. Joe let Joe Jr. take control of the plane and enjoyed coaching him as they made their way north. Father and son stopped in Ketchikan, Juneau, Anchorage, and Fairbanks, spending a day or two in each community. There was excitement at each stop when the local people saw a Seabee for the first time and then realized Joe Crosson was flying it. Receptions for Crosson and his plane were held in each town as they traveled north.

While Crosson attended to business in several other Alaska communities, he left Joe Jr. with friends in Fairbanks. On July 16, the boy celebrated his sixteenth birthday. He realized he was now old enough to be eligible for jobs in the Territory, so he went down to the state employment office and applied for the first job that was offered. A few days later his father returned to Fairbanks and was surprised to hear of Joe Jr.'s new occupation. And no doubt more than one official at Alaska Airlines laughed when he learned that Joe Crosson had been hired to sweep out their hangar.

On another occasion, Joe took son Don along on a delivery flight. The pair picked up a little two-seat, 65-horsepower Taylorcraft at Portland, Oregon, for a ferry flight to Ketchikan. On the way, Joe let Don take the controls, telling his son, "Head for that mountain over

No doubt more than one official at Alaska Airlines laughed when he learned that Joe Crosson had been hired to sweep out their hangar.

▶ *Joe and Lillian and their children (left to right) Joe Jr., Bob, Sue, and Don are pictured together in the winter of 1948.*

there, I'm going to take a nap." Don flew diligently toward the mountain poking through the clouds. After a while the drone of the motor and warm sunshine proved too much for the teenager, and he too fell asleep.

Within seconds Joe was awake, and he roused his son. "You weren't supposed to fall asleep too," he told the surprised youngster. But there was no problem. Joe climbed back on top of the cloud layer, spotted the top of a familiar mountain, and completed the trip.

Back in Seattle, Northwest Air Service was experiencing difficulties. Although morale was generally high, a union organizer had persuaded the mechanics to vote in favor of the union and to go on strike. Northwest was not able to meet their demands. Pacific Airmotive, another aircraft service company, offered to buy Northwest

Air Service, and Joe and his partners accepted. Crosson then rented
another location at Boeing Field and started a new parts business.

On the morning of June 21, 1949, Crosson drove his son Joe Jr. to
Arctic Pacific Airlines, where the young man worked, and continued
on to his own office at Boeing Field. Joe Jr. worked all morning hauling
freight between the airport and Sears. While at Sears, he received an
urgent phone call ordering him back to the office.

Shortly after noon, Joe Crosson's old friend Clark Bassett rushed
to the Crosson home in Lake Forest Park with devastating news for
Lillian. Joe had been found on the floor of his office. He had died of a
massive heart attack. He was forty-six years old.

EPILOGUE

Seattle, 1949. A cloud of gloom descended over the Crosson house at Lake Forest Park. Joe was gone. For the first time in more than twenty years, Lillian felt alone. Family and friends tried to comfort her, but she was alone in spirit. In the morning, Joe had kissed her good-bye as he had a thousand times before. But this day, when he simply went to the office, not off to some unknown region of the Arctic, he did not return.

Joe Crosson's death was noted by the nation. *Time* and *Newsweek* magazines carried his obituary, and he was called the "Troubleshooter of the Arctic." On his national radio program, Arthur Godfrey featured Crosson and his accomplishments in the Alaskan skies.

Famed mountaineer Bradford Washburn proposed naming a peak for Joe Crosson. Washburn had spent more days on Mount McKinley than any man alive, and he knew very well of Joe's contribution to mountain flying and the understanding of McKinley. Washburn petitioned the U.S. Geological Survey to name a 12,800-foot peak near Mount McKinley in Joe's honor. The proposal was accepted, and Mount Crosson was named.

The first days after Joe's death were a blur for Lillian. Joe's sister Zelma and her husband Barney helped with funeral arrangements, and

Joe was put to rest in a cemetery near the family home. Lillian's sense of despair was overwhelming, and she didn't know what to do. Some words from Clark Bassett helped immensely.

Bassett was the man who drove the "getaway car" when Joe and Lillian left Fairbanks on their honeymoon. Joe's death was difficult for Clark, too. But seeing that Lillian had yet to accept the situation, he spoke firmly to her: "Lillian, buck up, you've got four kids to take care of." The simple statement hit home. With that honest admonishment from a longtime friend, Lillian began putting her life back together.

Joe Jr. was eighteen and headed for college at the University of Washington. The other three children also needed a strong mother. Don, at fifteen, was in high school, and eleven-year old Bob was still in elementary school. Three-year-old Susan couldn't understand where Daddy had gone.

Lillian had been a full-time housewife and mother for nearly twenty years, and Joe had taken care of the finances. Now for the first time, at the age of forty-one, she learned the details of their financial situation. What she found was not good. Joe's business dealings were largely based on month-to-month operations, with little room for error. As long as Joe was at the helm, trading in aircraft and parts, things worked smoothly. Those days were gone.

Lillian didn't have to make any immediate decisions, but it was clear she couldn't afford to stay in the large Lake Forest Park home indefinitely. Joe and Lillian had been providing a home and caring for Joe's parents, but now Zelma and Barney told her they could help Esler and Elizabeth Crosson if Lillian decided to move.

Lillian thought longingly of Fairbanks, the town that had been so good to the Crossons. Friends encouraged her to return. She had only a few hundred dollars, and no secure future. She was unskilled in the business world and had no career to fall back on. But she was Lillian Crosson, the strong-willed, independent woman with whom Joe had chosen to share his life, and she couldn't fail now.

About a year after Joe died, Lillian sold the Lake Forest Park house and disposed of the business at Boeing Field. She bought a small house on Lake Washington to make sure she had a place to live if she

"Lillian, buck up, you've got four kids to take care of." The simple statement hit home.

*Lillian eventually found
her principal career, and
it turned out to be closely
connected to the world of
aviation and travel that
she had known for so
many years. She started
a travel agency.*

needed it. She then bought a travel trailer, packed up Don, Bob, Susan, and the dog, and headed for Fairbanks, more than twenty-three hundred miles away at the end of a long gravel road called the Alcan Highway.

In Fairbanks, Lillian found a house and moved the family in. Her first job was selling polio insurance to local parents. It would still be years before an effective vaccine was developed for the dreaded childhood disease, and sadly, many parents in Alaska collected on the policies sold by Lillian.

Next, she sold display advertising in the first phone book in Fairbanks. She knew so many people in the business world that she single-handedly sold more ads than were sold in all of Anchorage, now a much larger city.

She met with Bill Snedden, publisher of the *Fairbanks Daily News-Miner*, about another possible job. He was looking for someone to supervise the rowdy group of boys who delivered the paper each afternoon. He told her he preferred to hire someone younger, "but since you have three sons, you know how to deal with these boys." She took the job and was a success at managing the boys—two of whom were her own sons.

She was hired away from the newspaper by the Fairbanks Chamber of Commerce, to serve as event organizer. Her talents in that job impressed the Seattle Chamber of Commerce, which enticed her to return to the larger city and work in the same capacity there.

Back in Seattle, Lillian eventually found her principal career, and it turned out to be closely connected to the world of aviation and travel that she had known for so many years. She started a travel agency. It seemed that Joe was again at her side, as one of his old friends stepped in to help: Lillian obtained the backing of World War I ace and Eastern Airlines founder Eddie Rickenbacker, and she founded Bon Voyage Travel.

Over the next thirty years, Lillian's agency grew from one small ticket counter in the downtown Bon Marché department store to an office in every Bon from Everett to Tacoma. She retired after more than three decades in the travel business.

Joe Jr. finished college in Washington and joined the Army as a pilot. After his military duty, he was hired as a pilot by a local airline that eventually became part of Delta Airlines. He flew for thirty-three years, often on the Alaska route, before his retirement. He and his wife had three children, and he enjoys the outdoors much as his father did.

Don, who looks very much like his father, shared Joe's love of Alaska and adventure. Don lived for many years in Alaska, operating a small grocery store in Seldovia and flying supplies to remote areas. Don and his wife, who had three children, now divide their time between Washington and Alaska and enjoy fishing, hunting, and flying.

Bob became a professor of geophysics at the University of Washington, renowned in his field. He didn't pursue aviation either professionally or privately. Bob shares his love of the outdoors with his wife and two sons. He enjoys cross-country skiing, and sailing in the San Juan Islands.

Susan married and devoted herself to raising her three children. She and her husband collect antiques, and one wall of their home is devoted to photos of her famous family: father Joe, mother Lillian, and aunt Marvel. Lillian says her daughter is very much like Joe, and Susan flashes her father's smile.

In 1969, after her children were raised and out on their own as adults, Lillian accepted a marriage proposal from Barney Frizell, who was married to Joe's sister Zelma before her death. Barney and Lillian spent many happy years boating, fishing, traveling, and living in different parts of the world. Barney died in 1982.

Lillian still lives in her house on Lake Washington and keeps in close touch with her children, grandchildren, and great-grandchildren. She remembers her time with Joe as the best years of her life.

She was Lillian Crosson, the strong-willed, independent woman with whom Joe had chosen to share his life, and she couldn't fail now.

The Aircraft of Joe Crosson's Career

The following aircraft were important in Joe Crosson's career, with each plane
marking a milestone in the advancement of aviation in Alaska. With the exception of the
Sikorsky S-42 and S-43, he flew them all during his years in Alaska and in Seattle.

Sikorsky S-42 and Lockheed Electra. A Sikorsky S-42 seaplane passes over a beautifully polished Lockheed Electra on the ramp at Juneau. Both aircraft played significant roles in bringing aviation in Alaska into the modern era.

Lockheed Lodestar. The Lodestar was put into service on Pacific Alaska Airways' fledgling land-based service from Seattle to Alaska.

Consolidated Fleetster. The Fleetster could carry a larger payload and more passengers than the Fairchild 71, but the model never lived up to the expectations of Pacific Alaska Airways.

Pilgrim. The large Pilgrim was tough, dependable, capable of hauling bulky cargo into remote airstrips, and well-suited for bush operations.

Fairchild 71. The Fairchild 71 had unique folding wings that could be swung back against the fuselage with the removal of four bolts, allowing several planes to be stored in limited space.

Fokker Universal. During the summer of 1928, Joe Crosson delivered and flew Fokker Universals on floats throughout Canada.

Standard J-1. The Standard in the foreground was outfitted with a custom cabin designed and built by A. A. Bennett in Fairbanks. Crosson narrowly escaped death in the cabin craft when it caught fire in midair.

Super Swallow. The Super Swallow was a regular in Crosson's logbook. The plane survived a dunking in the Kuskokwim River to take him through the Brooks Range to Barrow during 1927.

Stearman C2B. A Stearman C2B, one of the trustiest biplanes in Alaska, operated from Mount McKinley's Muldrow Glacier in 1932.

Sikorsky S-43. The S-43 amphibian was the first airplane used by Pacific Alaska Airways for testing scheduled service from the continental United States to Alaska.

Waco 9. A Waco 9 with damaged propeller sits on a gravel bar. Whenever possible, spare propellers were carried on flights in the Alaska bush.

Sikorsky S-42 and Lockheed Electra

Lockheed Lodestar

Consolidated Fleetster

Pilgrim

Super Swallow

Fairchild 71

Stearman C2B

Fokker Universal

Sikorsky S-43

Standard J-1

Waco 9

Principal Airlines Associated with the Career of Joe Crosson

Listed years indicate the year in which a company was founded (except as noted for Alaska Southern Airways)

1923
Farthest-North Airplane Company
Formed in March 1923 following
   meetings with Fairbanks citizens
   and schoolteacher Ben Eielson.
Directors:
   Richard C. Wood, president of
      First National Bank of Fairbanks
   William F. Thompson, editor of
      Fairbanks Daily News-Miner

1924
**Alaska Aerial Transportation
   Company**
Formed in Fairbanks by Alaska Railroad
   conductor James S. Rodebaugh, with
   money made in trading furs.
Owner: James S. "Jimmy" Rodebaugh

1924-1925
Fairbanks Airplane Corporation
Formed by merger of Farthest-North
   Airplane Company and Alaska Aerial
   Transportation Company in
   December 1924; first operated in 1925.
Manager: James S. "Jimmy" Rodebaugh
Chief Pilot: Noel Wien, 1924
Chief Pilot: A. A. Bennett, 1925
Chief Pilot: Joe Crosson, 1926-1927

1926
Bennett-Rodebaugh Company
Formed in Fairbanks after Rodebaugh
   was replaced as Fairbanks Airplane
   Corporation manager.
Manager: James S. "Jimmy" Rodebaugh
Chief Pilot: A. A. Bennett

1926
Anchorage Air Transport
Incorporated in Anchorage, December 1926
President and General Manager:
   A. A. Shonbeck

1927
Nome Airplane Company
Formed in Nome, May 1927
Investor and Pilot: Noel Wien
Investors: Gene Miller, photographer,
   and Harry Phillips, merchant
Mechanic: Ralph Wien
The company was restructured later in
   1927, when Miller sold his interest
   and other investors provided working
   capital to expand the operation. In
   September 1927, the company became
   Wien Alaska Airways.

1927
Wien Alaska Airways
Formed in Nome (from Nome Airplane
   Company), September 1927
President and Chief Pilot: Noel Wien
Vice-President and Pilot: Ralph Wien

1929
Alaskan Airways
Formation of company announced
   August 1929. Funds provided by
   Delaware-based Aviation Corporation
   of America (parent company of
   American Airways). Company took
   over the assets of Bennett-Rodebaugh
   Company, Wien Alaska Airways, and
   Anchorage Air Transport.
Chief Pilot: Joe Crosson, 1929-1930
General manger: Ben Eielson, 1929-1930
General Manager: Joe Crosson, 1930-1932
Operations Manager: Charles L.
   Thompson, 1929-1930
Operations Manager: Arthur W.
   Johnson, 1930-1932
Operations Manager: Joe Crosson, 1932

1930
Pacific International Airways
Incorporated in Anchorage, August 1930,
   by Alonzo Cope and Frank Dorbandt.

1932
Pacific Alaska Airways
Formed as a subsidiary of Pan American
   Airways of New York, combining
   assets of Alaskan Airways and
   Pacific International Airways.
   Headquartered originally in
   Fairbanks, later moved to Seattle
General Manager: Lyman Peck,
   1932-1937
Operations Manager: Joe Barrows, 1932
Operations Manager: Joe Crosson,
   1933-1938
General Manager: Joe Crosson,
   1938-1941

1932
Alaska Southern Airways
Formed in 1932 when it took over the
   assets of Alaska Washington Airways,
   which operated out of Seattle
   beginning in 1929. Alaska Southern
   Airways was purchased in 1934 by
   Pacific Alaska Airways for Alaska
   Southern's facilities at Juneau,
   Ketchikan, and Seattle.

1941
**Alaska Division of Pan American
   Airways System**
Pacific Alaska Airways was reorganized
   as the Alaska Division of Pan Am,
   May 1941.
Division Manager: Joe Crosson
   1941-1944

Consolidation of Principal Airlines Associated with the Career of Joe Crosson

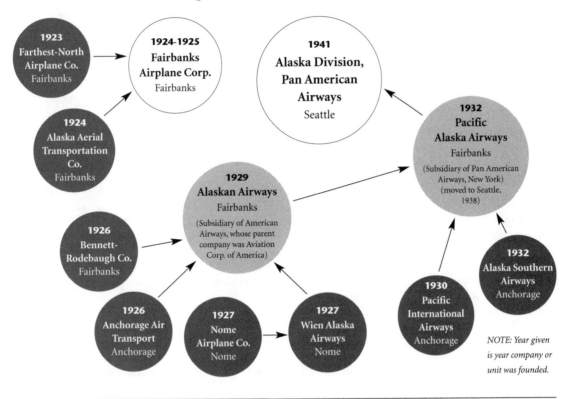

Radio/weather Stations Built and Maintained by Pacific Alaska Airways

The following radio/weather stations were opened in the years indicated, and they remained staffed
and in operation while Pacific Alaska Airways had mail or passenger routes in the region.

1932
Fairbanks

1934
Koyuk

1935
Burwash, Yukon
Juneau
McGrath
Nome
Nulato
Skagway
Taku
Whitehorse, Yukon

1936
Flat
Lake Minchumina

1937
Bethel

1938
Ketchikan
Seattle
Tanacross
Tanana

1940
Prince George, B.C.

1941
Dease Lake, B.C.
Takla, B.C.

Primary Aircraft of Joe Crosson's Career

Joe Crosson piloted a wide variety of aircraft during his long career, including the following planes. The rated horsepower for each engine was given in various publications, but it is difficult to confirm these figures because most engines had several different models, each with a variety of horsepower ratings. Also, engine modifications often changed the horsepower.

Curtiss JN-4D Jenny
Open-cockpit biplane; passengers in front, pilot in rear.
Primary construction, wood and fabric.
Rebuilt from surplus N-9 Navy floatplane by Joe Crosson and his sister Marvel in San Diego, California.
Engine: Curtiss OX-5, 90 horsepower, water-cooled V-8.

Curtiss JN-4D Jenny
Open-cockpit biplane; passengers in front, pilot in rear.
Primary construction, wood and fabric.
Flown by Joe Crosson in Fairbanks; same type of plane as flown by Joe and Marvel Crosson in San Diego.
Engine: Curtiss OX-5, 90 horsepower, water-cooled V-8. Engine changed March 1927 to Hispano-Suiza , 150 horsepower, water-cooled V-8.

Standard S-1
Open-cockpit biplane; passengers in front, pilot in rear. Passenger cabin enclosed by pilot/mechanic A. A. Bennett, March 1926.
Primary construction, wood and fabric.
One of the S-1 craft flown by Crosson.
Engine: Hispano-Suiza, 150 horsepower, water-cooled V-8. Engine changed March 1926 to Hispano-Suiza Model E, 180 horsepower, water-cooled V-8.

Standard S-1
Open-cockpit biplane; passengers in front, pilot in rear.
Primary construction, wood and fabric.
One of the S-1 craft flown by Crosson.
Engine: Hispano-Suiza, 150 horsepower, water-cooled V-8.

Waco Model 9
Open-cockpit biplane; passengers in front, pilot in rear.
Primary construction, steel tubing and fabric.
Crosson flew three of these planes.
Engine No. 1, Curtiss OX-5, 90 horsepower, water-cooled V-8.
Engine No. 2, Curtiss OXX6, 90 horsepower, water-cooled V-8.
Engine No. 3, Hispano-Suiza Model E2, 180 horsepower, water-cooled V-8.

Super Swallow
Open-cockpit biplane; passengers in front, pilot in rear.
Primary construction, steel tubing and fabric.
Engine: Hispano-Suiza Model E, 180 horsepower, water-cooled V-8.

Fokker Universal
Enclosed-cabin monoplane.
Primary construction, wood and fabric.
Engine: Wright J-5 Whirlwind, air-cooled radial.

Fairchild 71
Enclosed cabin monoplane; folding wings.
Primary construction, steel tubing and fabric.
Engine: Wright J-6 Wasp 300, air-cooled radial.

Stearman C2B
Open-cockpit biplane; passengers in front, pilot in rear.
Primary construction, steel tubing and fabric.
Engine: Wright J-5 Whirlwind, air-cooled radial.

Consolidated Fleetster
Enclosed cabin monoplane.
Primary construction, steel tubing and fabric.
Engine: Cyclone F, air-cooled radial.

Lockheed Electra 10
Enclosed-cabin monoplane; ten-passenger.
Primary construction, full metal.
Two engines: Wright J-6 Wasp, 450 horsepower, air-cooled radial.

Republic Seabee
Enclosed-cabin amphibian; four-passenger.
Primary construction, full metal.
Engine: Franklin, 180 horsepower, air-cooled, horizontal opposed six-cylinder.

List of Airplanes from Joe Crosson's Logbook

This list includes the great variety of aircraft that Joe Crosson recorded in his logbook, although it does not reflect all the variants of each model that he flew.

Aircraft	Engines	Aircraft	Engines
Curtiss JN-4D Jenny	Curtiss OX5; Hispano-Suiza	Boeing plane	Wright J-6 Wasp 300
Standard S-1	Hispano-Suiza; Wright J-5 Whirlwind	*(specific model not noted in log)*	
Waco Model 9	Curtiss OX5; Curtiss OXX6; Hispano-Suiza	Travel Air	Wright J-5 Whirlwind
		Swallow	Kinner; Wright J-6 Wasp
Super Swallow	Hispano-Suiza	Waco Model 10	Wright J-5 Whirlwind
Stinson Detroiter	Wright J-4B	Zenith Z-6	Not known
Fokker F.III	BMW	Stinson SB-1	Wright J-5 Whirlwind
Ryan M1	Hispano-Suiza	Fairchild 71	Wright J-6 Wasp 300
International	Curtiss OX5	Stearman C2B	Wright J-5 Whirlwind
Breese	Wright J-5 Whirlwind	Loening Amphibian	Wright J-6 Wasp
Eaglerock	Curtiss OX5	Pilgrim	Wright J-6 Wasp
Travel Air	Curtiss OX5; Challenger; Wright J-5 Whirlwind; Wright J-6	Consolidated Fleetster	Cyclone
		Ford	Cyclone
		(Tri-Motor converted to single engine)	
Fokker Universal	Wright J-5 Whirlwind	Lockheed Electra 10	Wright J-6 Wasp
Ford Tri-Motor	Wright J-5 Whirlwind (3 engines)	Douglas DC-3	Cyclone
		Lockheed Lodestar	Pratt & Whitney 1830
Junkers F-13	L-6 (uncertain)	Ercoupe	Continental
Aero Marine	Mercedes	Republic Seabee	Franklin
Fokker F-7 Tri-Motor	Wright J-5 Whirlwind (3 engines)	Stinson	Lycoming
		Taylorcraft	Continental
Flamingo	Siemons; Haskle	Cessna	Jacobs
Lockheed Vega	Wright J-5 Whirlwind; Wright J-6 Wasp	AT-6	Wright Wasp H

Honors and Awards to Joe Crosson

1927 Pioneers of Alaska, honorary membership.

1935 Oklahoma National Guard special commission.

1937 Alaska Aeronautics and Communications Commission appointment.

1937 Explorers Club of New York induction.

1943 Men With Wings trophy recipient.

1946 War Department Operations Analyst commendation.

1949 Mount Crosson named in Alaska Range.

1949-50 Streets named for Crosson in Fairbanks, Anchorage, and San Diego.

1953 Crosson Field dedicated in Sterling, Colorado (honoring Joe Crosson and Marvel Crosson).

1958 Plaque placed in Pioneer Square, Fairbanks, Alaska.

1982 Curtiss OX-5 Hall of Fame induction, San Francisco.

1984 Aviation Pioneer Award, Seattle, Washington.

2002 Alaska Aviators Hall of Fame induction, Anchorage, Alaska.

INDEX

ABOUT THE AUTHOR

DIRK TORDOFF was born in the Territory of Alaska and has always loved Alaska history and flying. He earned a Master of Arts degree in Northern Studies from the University of Alaska Fairbanks and has published several articles on Alaska aviation history. When he's not working as a film archivist at the University of Alaska Library in Fairbanks, he enjoys being outdoors, fishing with his wife and two sons, and tinkering in the garage on classic cars and trucks.